The Vanishing Border

THE VANISHING BORDER

A Photographic Journey
Along Our Frontier with Mexico

Brent Ashabranner

Photographs by Paul Conklin

DODD, MEAD & COMPANY
New York

Designed by Joy Taylor

1 2 3 4 5 6 7 8 9 10

Maps by Heather Saunders

Library of Congress Cataloging-in-Publication Data

Ashabranner, Brent K., date
The vanishing border.

Bibliography: p.
Includes index.
Summary: Describes, in text and photographs, some of the unique
characteristics of the 2000 mile border region between Mexico and the
United States, a region that blends the cultures from both sides of the
border.   1. Mexican-American Border Region—Description and travel—
Juvenile literature.   2. Mexican-American Border Region—Description
and travel—Views—Juvenile literature.   3. Ashabranner, Brent K., date
—Juvenile literature.   4. Conklin, Paul—Juvenile literature.

[1.   Mexican-American Border Region]   I.   Conklin, Paul.
II.   Title.
F787.A84   1987   979   87-16910
ISBN 0-396-08900-3

For David and Peter

Contents

Acknowledgments

THE BOOK that came out of our several visits to the border would have been impossible without the help of many people. For their time, patience, and understanding we thank all those whose names appear in the pages ahead. In addition, and at the risk of some unintentional omission, we also wish to express our appreciation to a number of other persons who gave abundantly of their time and knowledge of the border.

Jose Muniz, Deputy Director of the Chicano Federation of San Diego County, and Hector Culver, also of San Diego, shared their deep knowledge of Mexican-American life in that area. Les and Linda Davis, New Mexico ranchers, opened other ranch doors in the state for us. Louis R. (Ray) Sadler, Director, Joint Border Research Institute, Las Cruces, New Mexico, met with us on three separate occasions to discuss a wide range of border issues. Phil Neighbors, West Texas Chamber of Commerce, Abilene, helped us in many ways, as did professional photographer, David Kennedy, who lives in Austin, Texas.

Our Texas travels and inquiries were enriched by the assistance of Joe Old, reporter for the *El Paso Herald Post*; George N. Rodriguez, Jr., Director of the Govenor's El Paso Regional Office; and Elizabeth Rogers, assistant public defender, El Paso. Our old El Paso friend, Al Velarde, Regional Director, Migration and Refugee Services, U.S. Catholic Conference, gave us wise counsel, as always;

Margie Sapien, also of Migration and Refugee Services, El Paso, helped with information and introductions. Abelardo Muniz, a graduate student at the University of Texas, El Paso, when we met him, was a thoughtful and instructive companion on one of our visits to Juárez.

In Del Rio, Texas, Joan Luttrell of the local Chamber of Commerce provided us with useful background. In Laredo, Texas, Adriana Martinez, Laredo Development Council, and others from that agency showed us industrial activities both in Laredo and Nuevo Laredo, Mexico. Our days in the lower Rio Grande Valley were made more profitable by Rafael Guerra, Texas Migrant Council, Rio Grande City, who also helped us two years earlier in our work on *Dark Harvest: Migrant Farmworkers in America*.

The U.S. Border Patrol Agent on the jacket is H.M. (Mike) Calvert of El Paso; we salute him for his years of outstanding service to the Border Patrol.

We are indebted to Congressman Romano Mazzoli and to Ann Cumming, formerly of Mr. Mazzoli's office, for help with research materials necessary to this book. Congressman Mazzoli has worked extensively on immigration legislation since the early 1980s and was a sponsor of the new immigration bill passed by the Congress in October, 1986.

Finally, we would like to thank the U.S. Office of the International Boundary and Water Commission, El Paso, for information about the length of the border in its entirety and in its various state segments.

I

A BORDER
LIKE
NO OTHER

U.S. HIGHWAY 8 cuts its scorched and lonely way through California's Imperial Valley, paralleling the Mexican border only a few miles away. On a July day when the temperature outside our car was 110 degrees, Paul and I traveled this famous old route, known to pre-Civil War stagecoach drivers and their passengers as the Butterfield Trail. We were on our way to Yuma, Arizona, and as we neared the state line, we crossed the All American Canal. This 200-foot-wide canal delivers up to 15,000 cubic feet of water a second to the Imperial Valley and has helped create an agricultural miracle in the desert.

Paul decided we should have a picture and pulled off on a sandy shoulder a few hundred feet past the canal. He was taking his photographic equipment out of the trunk—we could not have been stopped for more than a minute—when a California Highway Patrol car pulled up behind us. The lone officer got out quickly, glanced in the car at me, then focused his attention on Paul.

"Are you having trouble?" he asked.

"No trouble," Paul said. "I want to get a picture of the canal."

The officer stood beside his patrol car, carefully alert. He was polite but firm. "Emergency stopping only on this highway," he said.

"It will just take me a minute," Paul said.

The officer shook his head, but Paul is not easily put off when his mind is on taking pictures. "I'm a professional photographer," he said. "My friend and I are gathering material for a book about the border."

I got out of the car, and the officer shifted his attention to include me as well as Paul. I handed him a brochure that our publisher puts out about our work and also a copy of *Dark Harvest*, a recent book of ours about migrant farmworkers.

"We spent a day with the Border Patrol in the Chula Vista Sector," I told the officer and named two Border Patrol officers we had been with. Mentioning names, I discovered long ago, may do no good in a situation like this but seldom does any harm.

The Highway Patrolman seemed to relax just a bit. "I know them," he said. He glanced at the brochure and the book.

"Okay," he said to Paul, "take your picture. But there's another picture your border book should have."

The officer pointed and at first I didn't see anything but sand, scrub bushes, and a barbed-wire fence. "The fence?" I asked, puzzled.

"The plastic containers," he said.

Only then did I notice them, a number of empty one-gallon plastic containers, some half-buried in the sand, strung out for perhaps a hundred yards along the fence and highway.

"Is this a dump area?" I asked, wondering why the officer thought some discarded plastic containers—they looked like milk containers to me—would make a good border picture.

"Not the kind of dump area you're talking about," he said. "Those containers were thrown there by illegals who have crossed the border from Mexico. That gallon of water gets them through the desert. When they reach this spot, they either fill up their jugs from the canal and go on or they throw them away because they've arranged for someone to pick them up. Sometimes they throw away everything they're carrying and run, if the Border Patrol or Highway Patrol surprises them. This place where the canal and the highway come together is a favorite spot for illegals to head for after they've crossed the border."

And then I understood. I stared at the officer. "You thought we had stopped here to pick up illegal aliens!" I said. "That's why you pulled in behind us so fast."

The patrolman permitted himself a small smile. "Let's just say I was curious about why you picked this place to stop," he said.

Empty one-gallon plastic containers discarded along the fence.

Paul took a picture of the plastic containers and then trudged off through the sand to photograph the canal. I pulled my notebook out of my pocket and continued to talk to the Highway Patrolman, a nice guy whose name was Jim Hartley and who had seen a great deal in his years of working this border highway.

IN GATHERING material for a book, I always find that some moments haunt my memory, some faces are unforgettable, some scenes linger in my mind long after the book has been written. This book about the U.S.-Mexican border country produced many such memories: a young woman in a Mexicali factory, recently from a village deep in Mexico, showing us proudly how she helps assemble computers; the pale, flickering ghost image of a smuggler caught

California Highway Patrolman J. W. Hartley.

in the eye of a Border Patrol infrared night telescope; a New Mexico border rancher looking at the land made green by heavy summer rains and saying, "It sure is purty. This country is wearing its Sunday clothes."

But memory is a curious thing. The image which has stayed with me most vividly is that of empty plastic containers lying in the hot sand of the Imperial Valley desert. Each container represented a human being who for whatever reason was desperate to enter the United States, so desperate that he, or she, would cross a desert with only a gallon of water. I still wonder how many of those people eluded the Border Patrol. I wonder how many found what they were looking for on this side of the border.

I remember a Border Patrol agent who had a feeling for metaphor. "It's a border of dreams," he said, "and some nightmares."

6

One thing is certain: no other international border is like the U.S.-Mexican border. Nowhere else on this earth does a rich, highly industrialized country share such a long, open, easily crossed border with a large, poor, less-developed country. And an open border it is. In 1986 the Border Patrol made 1.8 million apprehensions of illegal aliens, over 90 percent of whom had entered the United States by crossing the Mexican border. No one knows how many hundreds of thousands successfully avoided the Border Patrol.

But during the same year of 1986, over 200 *million* people crossed legally from Mexico into the United States—dayworkers, shoppers, immigrants, tourists— many making multiple entries, of course. The great border crossing points like Tijuana and Juárez and some of the smaller ones like Nogales and Nuevo Laredo are rivers of human beings, flowing both ways.

Another thing is certain: Mexico, during the rest of this century and beyond, is going to have an impact on American lives that would have seemed impossible a generation ago. In 1940, with a population of 20 million, Mexico was taken for granted as "our little neighbor to the south." Today it is a nation of 85 million people. In less than twenty years, it will be 115 million, one of the fastest growing national populations in the world. Only the foolish or ignorant take this Latin-American giant for granted any longer.

We are tied together. Mexicans need jobs that are available in the United States. U.S. industries, particularly agriculture, want workers who will accept low wages. Mexico needs U.S. markets for its farm and mineral products. The United States needs oil, and Mexico has oil, estimated reserves of 70 billion barrels. More than anything, the United States wants a politically and economically stable Mexico that will not be drawn into the revolutionary turmoil that grips much of Central America.

"The real issue in Central America is Mexico," says Bruce Babbitt, former Governor of Arizona. "It is the ultimate domino…and it is right on our border."

Alfred Stepan, dean of the School of International and Public Affairs at Columbia University, has written: "Certainly—because of our capacity for mutual destruction—the Soviet Union is the No. 1

United States Border Inspection Station, El Paso, Texas.

country in the world for us to pay attention to. But Mexico is No. 2."

Former assistant secretary of state for Latin-American affairs William D. Rogers, writing in the *Washington Post*, had this to say: "If the United States has one truly special relationship with another country, that country is Mexico. A nation can choose its friends, but not its neighbors. We and Mexico are fated to live together.... We had best learn to exist side by side, with civility and understanding. What injures Mexico does damage to our own national interests as well."

Decisions made in Washington and Mexico City will profoundly affect whether we "exist side by side with civility and understanding." But where those words have immediate impact and everyday importance is in the twenty-five counties in California, Arizona, New Mexico, and Texas and the thirty-five *municipios* in six Mexican states that form the two thousand-mile-long border zone. Year after year the region is becoming increasingly interknit, both culturally and economically, border notwithstanding.

The San Diego merchant who counts heavily on shoppers from Tijuana, the Chihuahua rancher who sells his cattle in Texas and New Mexico, the Arizona citrus grower who needs workers from Mexico, the Brownsville schoolteacher who has more students from Matamoros than Brownsville in his class, the Mexican family with brothers and sisters living on both sides of the border—all of these people and millions like them ultimately will have the most to say about how our two countries will exist side by side.

USUALLY, before Paul and I embark on a book together, we talk about it for a long time. We want to make sure we both are deeply interested in the subject, satisfying ourselves that there is need for a book—or another book—on the subject and that we have something to offer. But this book about the U.S.-Mexican border was different. We just knew, without much talk, that we were going to do it.

Three of our previous books—*The New Americans*, *Dark Harvest*, and *Children of the Maya*—dealt in some way with the border country. It had been on our minds for a long time. One day I called Paul and said, "When can you be ready to go back to the border?"

Paul spends much of his time photographing politicians in Washington, D.C., press conferences, but he would infinitely rather be on the road with his cameras.

"Tomorrow," he said.

In fact, it was a month before we boarded a flight at D.C.'s National Airport and headed for San Diego, the largest U.S. city in the border zone.

II

THE DESERT BORDER

CALIFORNIA
ARIZONA
NEW MEXICO

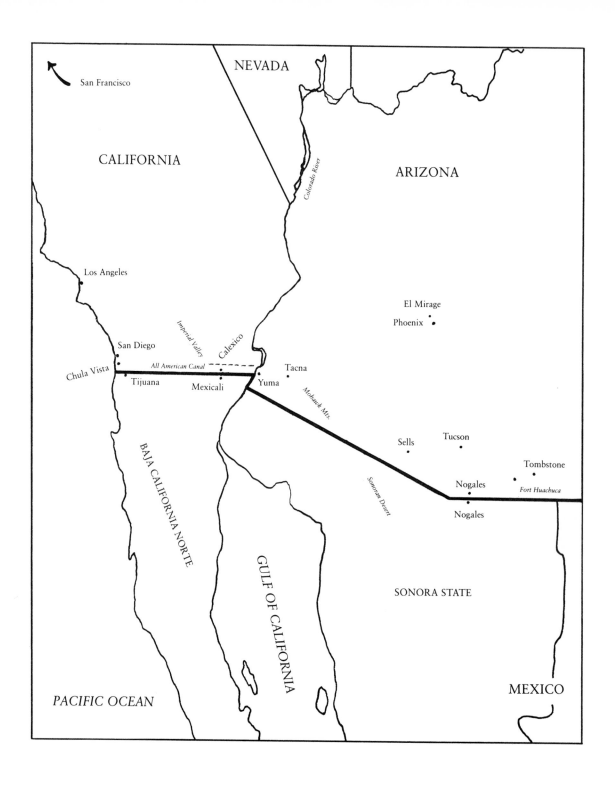

In EXACT measure, our border with Mexico is 1,952 miles long and stretches from the Gulf of Mexico to the Pacific Ocean. The border as we know it today was created by the Treaty of Guadalupe Hidalgo, which concluded the War with Mexico in 1848. Under the treaty's terms, Mexico gave up more than two-fifths of its territory, comprising much of the present states of California, Arizona, and New Mexico. For this vast expanse of land, Mexico received a payment of $3 million. Mexico also recognized U.S. sovereignty over Texas, which had declared its independence from Mexico in 1836. The Gadsden Purchase in 1853 added a final strip of land in extreme southern New Mexico and Arizona south of the Gila River.

The Rio Grande forms the entire boundary between Texas and Mexico. The river snakes its way south and east for 1,254 miles—almost two-thirds of the border's length—until it flows into the Gulf twenty miles east of Brownsville. Although it provides a clear, distinct, well-known division between Mexico and the United States, it is not much of a barrier. Small boats and swimmers find it little challenge; in many places, people wade across.

The border that separates Mexico from California, Arizona, and New Mexico has no river to define it. Most of its 698-mile length is marked by nothing more than a barbed-wire fence that in some places has fallen down. Only in urban areas where Mexican and U.S. cities exist side by side—Mexicali and Calexico, for example, or the two Nogales—do sturdier chain link fences appear.

In this part of the West and Southwest the real barrier is the desert, stark mountains, and arid plains through which the border runs. *Jornada de la Muerte*—the Journey of Death—early Spanish explorers called the border area of the Colorado Desert in California. In Arizona and New Mexico the border crosses the inhospitable Sonoran and Chihuahuan deserts.

But in this seemingly harsh and uninviting terrain, human imagination, determination, and hard work have created cities, irrigated farms, citrus orchards, and cattle ranches. And, in fact, deserts and mountains have proved to be no more a barrier to people on the move than the river that separates Texas and Mexico.

Gateway

"WELCOME to Paradise" said the tourist guidebook in my San Diego motel room, and it went on to describe paradise. San Diego has ideal weather, major league baseball and football, sixty-seven golf courses, the world's largest zoo, and Sea World where Shamu, a two-ton killer whale, is the star performer. It has miles of fine beaches, good swimming, surfing, waterskiing, and sailing. It has some of the best seafood and Mexican restaurants in the world, and great walking tours through Old Town where you can see the beginning of California history.

Paul came over from his room, his camera bag slung over his shoulder.

"Let's go see Shamu, the killer whale," I said.

Paul does not have a huge sense of humor when he is getting ready to take pictures. He glanced at his watch. He went to the window and looked up at the sun. Paul never stops thinking about light.

"We're due at the Border Patrol in half an hour," he said. "Let's go."

Our appointment was at Chula Vista Station, one of seven stations in the San Diego Border Patrol Sector. The San Diego Sector includes San Diego County and parts of Orange and Riverside counties to the north. This sector shares sixty-six miles of border with the Mexican state of Baja California. There are nine Border Patrol sectors on the U.S.-Mexico border, which means that the other eight sectors have to patrol 1,882 miles. But in the case of the San Diego Sector, the number of miles has nothing to do with the work load.

While Paul battled the freeway in our rented Mercury, I reviewed the information I had already collected. For years San Diego County has been the main gateway for illegal aliens entering the United States from Mexico. Every night they pour across the border by the thousands, mostly young men but women, too, and sometimes entire families.

San Diego is one of California's largest metropolitan areas, with thousands of service jobs in restaurants, hotels and motels, and more thousands in industries like garment manufacturing, food processing, and building construction. Just thirteen miles away on the Mexican side of the border is Tijuana, a tourist and manufacturing city of more than a million people. It attracts hundreds of thousands of people from all over Mexico, many of whom continue on to the United States.

San Diego and Tijuana are powerful people magnets. They are also the gateway to Los Angeles, San Francisco, and California's vast agricultural industry. Two figures from government studies are shocking—(1) Over 35 percent of all illegal aliens arrested along the entire U.S.-Mexican border have been apprehended in the San Diego Sector; (2) Almost 50 percent of all illegal aliens in the United States live in California. Los Angeles alone contained one-third of all illegal aliens counted in the 1980 U.S. census. How many illegal aliens are in the United States? No one knows, but informed estimates run between 3 and 6 million.

Why are illegal aliens, mostly Mexicans, coming to the United States in unprecedented numbers? That question is easier to answer. Since 1982, Mexico has been in a severe economic slump caused by falling oil prices. Millions of Mexicans are unemployed or underemployed. The falling value of the peso has made farming a starvation business. In addition, Mexico has a booming population, with almost a million young men and women entering the job market every year. For many who have lost their jobs, who have never had a job, or who cannot make a living farming, the only alternative is to try to come to the United States and find work.

SUPERVISORY Border Patrol Agent Ed Pyeatt was waiting for us in the Chula Vista headquarters building. My first question to Ed was, "Is it as bad as what we read in the papers?"

Ed put a piece of paper in my hand. "Look at that," he said.

The paper was a year-by-year list of the number of illegal aliens who had been caught in the San Diego Sector over the past twenty years. In every year (the government fiscal year) but four the number caught had increased, some years by as much as forty to fifty thousand. The first and last figures on the list astonished me. In 1965 the number of illegal aliens caught was 6,558. In 1986, with three months to go in the fiscal year, the figure was almost half a million and would surely go over six hundred thousand.

"That's a hundred times more than you caught in 1965," I said. "It's hard to believe."

"Believe it," Ed said. "Twenty years ago I got a special award for catching seven illegals in one night. Seven!"

He laughed at the absurdity of that number today.

"How many don't you catch?" I asked. "How many get through?"

Ed shook his head. "No way to know," he said. "Some think it's two for every one caught, some say more. I'm not sure it makes any difference how many we catch. They sign an I-274 Voluntary Return form. We load them in buses and send them back across the border. The ones that really want to get through will try again and keep trying until they make it."

Ed quickly sketched for us the resources of the San Diego Sector: 748 Border Patrol agents, 25 antismuggling officers, 48 detention officers. They are backed up by electronic technicians and radio operators, a data center, and an air operations branch. Air operations has two fixed-wing aircraft and three helicopters.

"We do a good job with our resources," Ed said, with a touch of pride. He thought for a moment, then added quietly, "But illegal entry is out of control."

"You Can't Stop the Tide"

ED PYEATT TURNED us over to Supervisory Border Patrol Agent R. J. Miller, who told us to call him Bob. Before we set out in Bob's Ram Charger for a look at the border, he took us to the big cinderblock "staging" building in the Chula Vista Station compound. Here are kept apprehended illegal aliens who cannot be immediately returned across the border.

"Mostly OTMs," Bob said.

OTM is Border Patrol shorthand for Other Than Mexican. The great majority of OTMs are from El Salvador, Guatemala, and Nicaragua. They cannot be sent back to Mexico because they are not Mexican citizens. Even if they sign voluntary return forms, arrangements must be made to fly them back to their countries. They almost never have money to buy their own return tickets. Most OTMs ask for political asylum and will stay in the United States until an immigration judge hears their cases. That may take weeks or months just to schedule.

"Do you get many OTMs from countries other than Central America?" I asked one of the detention officers.

He nodded. "Last year we caught undocumented OTMs from sixty-eight countries. Even countries like China, Egypt, and Norway. One from Vietnam. And lots from South American countries. The San Diego Sector caught over fourteen thousand last year."

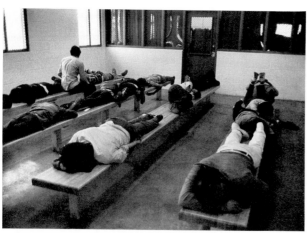

Recently caught aliens.

Aliens in detention, mostly OTMs from Central America.

I had been in Border Patrol detention facilities before, and it was no more fun now than it had been then. The recently caught aliens at the Chula Vista Station were exhausted. They were either sleeping on the wooden benches or too discouraged to sit up. Most of them had walked a thousand miles through Mexico to get to the United States. They had spent what little money they and their families had been able to scrape together for their journey. They had probably been caught within fifteen minutes after crossing the border. For them it was a border of broken dreams.

AFTER THE SKYSCRAPERS and freeways of San Diego, we were not prepared for our first look at the border. Bob Miller drove his van along the rutted dirt tracks that the Border Patrol calls drag roads. We skirted the edge of steep, brush-filled canyons that Bob gave names like Dillon Canyon, Smuggler's Canyon, and Deadman's Canyon. These uninhabited, brush-covered canyons and hills are a part of San Diego County; the hills are crisscrossed with deep trails worn down over the years by tens of thousands of illegal border crossers.

We stopped at the head of one of the canyons and looked across into Mexico. The chain link border fence was less than a third of a mile away, flush against the shacks and slums of Tijuana. Through field glasses we could see groups of people bunched near the fence. In a flat area that the Border Patrol calls the "soccer field" a hundred or more people were gathered, although it would be two hours before the sun would go down behind the hills in Mexico.

"By dark there'll be a couple of thousand people on the soccer field," Bob said, "maybe more. And more than that strung out along the fence. Then they'll come."

And there would be no stopping them. We had heard about it, but now we could see for ourselves. They would pour into the canyons by the thousands. They would come in small groups and large groups. Some would come alone. Some would be led by "coyotes," guides who charged up to a hundred dollars a person for their services. In the dark, in the miles of brush-covered hills and canyons, trying to stop them would be a dangerous and futile game.

20

"We'll be waiting for them when they come out," Bob said.

Border Patrol agents are helped by seismic sensors buried in the main trails. When someone steps on a sensor, a light flashes on a control panel at headquarters. The information is radioed to patrol cars, and the agents know where to make their moves. Sometimes helicopters with searchlights join the search. The Border Patrol rounds up hundreds of aliens every night or forces them back into the canyons.

But hundreds or thousands get through every night. "It's like the tide," one officer said to me. "You can't stop the tide. Not with a few hundred men and a couple of choppers."

A bit farther on Bob stopped on the rim of Goat Canyon. "It's one of the bad spots for border bandits," he said.

Gangs of armed thugs prey on the illegal border crossers. They beat them, rob them, sometimes murder them. Some "coyotes" lead the people who have paid them directly to waiting bandits. Because border crossers are in the country illegally, they seldom go to the police to report what has happened to them.

"The Border Patrol and the San Diego Police Department have started a Border Crimes Task Force," Bob said, "but it's hard to do much that can help these poor people."

Bob drove us to Border Field State Park, which is where the U.S.-Mexican border begins on the Pacific Ocean. San Diegoans come to the park for swimming, picnicking, and bird-watching. On the Mexican side is Las Playas de Tijuana, a resort with many restaurants and hotels. During the bull-fighting season, May to September, crowds of people come to the Bullring-by-the-Sea in the resort town every Sunday.

The border fence comes right down to the beach, but the beach itself is free and open. No immigration or customs officers from either country are on duty. Americans can stroll into Las Playas de Tijuana and have a sandwich or a drink at a restaurant. Mexicans can walk down the beach in San Diego County. Today, so late in the afternoon, almost no one was at the park, but eight Mexicans with bags were sitting on the beach, just on the Tijuana side.

"It looks like an easy way for an illegal to get into California," I said.

Border Field State Park. The border begins here on the shore of the Pacific Ocean.

"Maybe," Bob said. "They try. Sometimes they put on swim-trunks and even carry surfboards and walk down the beach toward Imperial City, just like they're Americans out to have fun. But we watch farther down and turn most of them back."

We left the park and drove back to a canyon rim where two Border Patrol vehicles were stationed. It was almost twilight now, and an officer was setting up a big telescope in the bed of a pickup truck.

"Infrared night scope," he said, when he saw me watching him.

"Can you really see in the dark with that thing?" I asked.

He laughed. "Spot a two-legged coyote right down in the bottom of the canyon."

A radio crackled in one of the trucks, and I went over to listen. "Two getting ready to cross 117," a radio voice said. "Victor 148, can you get them?"

I couldn't hear Victor 148's answer, but I knew that Highway 117 is a busy road near the border that many illegals have to cross when they come out of the canyons. It wasn't ten minutes before another Border Patrol van swung in beside us. It was Victor 148 with the two illegals who had been spotted crossing the highway. They were Guatemalans, and they were dazed, hardly able to comprehend that within minutes of crossing the border, they were in the hands of the Border Patrol.

Through one of the officers I asked them why they had left Guatemala. They had been out of work for over a year, they said. They had hoped to get jobs in California and send money back to their families. I asked how long they had been traveling. Twenty days, they said, walking and riding buses, with little rest or sleep.

The Guatemalans asked what would happen to them. The officer explained their options. They could agree to be returned voluntarily or they could request a hearing before an immigration judge and appeal to be allowed to stay in the United States.

The officer was polite, even gentle, as he talked to the bewildered young men. I had observed the same quality in other Border Patrol agents in other places. They knew how to handle trouble-makers, but they seemed to bear no ill will toward most of the illegal aliens they captured.

Border Patrol agent with an infrared night telescope.

A Border Patrol agent talks with two Guatemalans who have just been apprehended crossing the border into San Diego County.

Two years ago Mike Calvert, a veteran Texas Border Patrol agent, had said to me: "Most of these illegals aren't bad people. They just want to get a job, work hard, and send money home to their families. If they could make a decent living in Mexico, there wouldn't be any illegal alien problem, at least not much of one."

I think Mike was expressing the feeling of most Border Patrol agents. Perhaps that is why the Border Patrol has such a high morale. In nine cases out of ten they are not dealing with criminals and if, as one agent said to me, they can just "keep the lid on," they will have fulfilled their mission.

"We Give You Our Children"

NOT SO MANY years ago, Tijuana was a seedy border town with a questionable reputation. Today it boasts that it is the most visited city in the world. A major growth of manufacturing plants and booming tourism have changed Tijuana completely and given it a great deal to boast about. It is a free port, and Avenida Revolución, one of the main shopping areas, has stores and specialty shops with bargains from all over the world.

Sports events are big in Tijuana. Besides the Bullring-by-the-Sea, bullfights are held in another arena, El Toreo de Tijuana. The famous Agua Caliente racetrack is here, and Mexican rodeos, called *charreadas*, take place every Sunday from May through September. Tourists by the millions pour into Tijuana through the U.S. Port of Entry at San Ysidro, just a few miles from San Diego.

We parked our car in the San Ysidro parking lot and walked across the border into Tijuana. There was no immigration check on either side. No passport is needed by U.S. citizens if their visit to Mexico is seventy-two hours or less. They make it easy to cross over and spend dollars.

26

We wanted to do some tourist things, but first we had to see people. Our good El Paso friend, Al Velarde, who seems to know everyone on the border concerned with Mexican migration, told us to begin in Tijuana with Monsignor Isidro Punte, and we made an appointment. When I talked on the phone to the Monsignor, I told him we had seen and heard about the Mexican migration from the U.S. side of the border; now we wanted to do the same from the Mexican side.

We hailed a taxi, and gave the driver the address of the Sacred Heart Church where Monsignor Punte has his office. The ride was a short one; when we arrived, Paul, in his best Spanish, asked the driver what the fare was.

"Fifty dollars," the driver said in English, and laughed at the expression on our faces. "Every tourist think Tijuana taxi driver is big crook, so I make joke. Five dollars."

We paid him five dollars for the ride and a dollar for the joke, and everyone was happy.

MONSIGNOR PUNTE had arranged to put us in the hands of Father Florencio Maria Rigoni, a priest who works directly with people migrating to Tijuana and the United States. But before we left the church, we talked briefly with the Monsignor, and I understood why Al Velarde had said we should start with him. He feels deeply about what is happening in his country, and the man is a pure poet.

In ten minutes' conversation, Monsignor Punte referred to the U.S.-Mexican border in these ways:

"...the northern gate of the Third World." He was talking about how the border has replaced Ellis Island as the door through which poor people from poor countries now enter the United States.

"...the gate of tragedy." This phrase came out as he described the grinding poverty of Mexico that is forcing men to leave their homes to seek work in the north.

"...the gate of abandoned people." People are not flowing across the border in such numbers because they want to, the Monsi-

Monsignor Isidro Punte.

gnor said, but rather because their governments do not care enough about what has happened to them.

"…the gate of hope." America was the symbol of hope for poor and oppressed Europeans a century ago, Monsignor Punte stated; now it is viewed that way by people of Latin-American countries.

"…the gate of tomorrow." What is happening today, Monsignor Punte believes, will force the United States and Mexico to a clearer and better understanding of each other in the future.

Monsignor Punte spoke of Mexicans' love of their families, their culture, their church. "We are held together by the glue which is love. Mexican men leave their families and their country not because they want to but because they have to. They return when they can. No matter where he is, a Mexican is proud that he is a Mexican. He values all those things that have made him a Mexican.

"The greatest tragedy," the Monsignor continued, "is that the children are left without fathers. Now too many villages in Mexico have only mothers and children and old people."

On the subject of the thousands of young men in their teens and early twenties who pour into Tijuana every month, the Monsignor said, "Many could find jobs in this city, but they believe tales of how much money they can make across the border. They want adventure and their *machismo*—their manliness—requires that they can say they have been to the United States. They say, 'Norte was our land. California was Mexican for a long time.' And so they go. To them we say, 'Go, children, but be careful and God bless you.' To the United States we say, 'We give you our children. Treat them well.'"

FATHER RIGONI appeared and whisked us away in an ancient Dodge. He is Italian, a member of the Scalabrini Order, whose purpose is to help migrants and people traditionally on the move. Before being assigned in Tijuana, Father Rigoni spent three years on merchant ships in the Pacific ministering to seamen.

His mission in Tijuana is to give help and give guidance to young men and women who come to Tijuana from all over Mexico and Central America. Most see this city as a temporary stop on their way

Father Florencio Maria Rigoni.

to the United States, but the priest hopes that many who come his way will stay on the Mexican side of the border.

Father Rigoni is supercharged with energy and talked steadily as he guided his car through the frightening Tijuana traffic. He spoke bitterly of some Mexican police who victimize border crossers, demanding as much as a hundred dollars before they will let the person cross. He talked about border bandits who are making the crossing a "hell" for all those unfortunate enough to fall into their hands.

"Sometimes these young people crawl back to Tijuana, robbed, beaten, half-dead," he said. "Then we try to take care of them. But if we can help them before that happens, it is so much better."

Father Rigoni took us to a building in downtown Tijuana where he and a small volunteer staff counsel the young people who come for guidance. They also arrange job training and help them find jobs. "We help sixty or seventy a month," he said. "Not many when thousands come to Tijuana every week, but it is a start."

We drove to an area of the city called Colonia Postal where Father Rigoni is pastor of San Filipe Church. He is building a hostel here where two hundred homeless people can eat, sleep, and keep clean. "We are begging and borrowing money and materials from everywhere to build this hostel," he said. "Soon it will be ready."

At the church we met Victor and Ramon, two young Nicaraguans who have been helped by Father Rigoni's program. Ramon is eighteen and left Nicaragua when he was sixteen with four other boys his age. I asked Ramon why he had left. "I did not like that government," he said, "and I did not want to be in that army."

Ramon and his friends came to Tijuana with the intention of crossing into the United States, but in Tijuana he met Victor, who introduced him to Father Rigoni. The priest persuaded Ramon to stay in Tijuana and helped him find a job. Now he is working as a welder for a goldsmith, learning a trade in jewelry-making and earning a living. Ramon talked his four friends from Nicaragua into staying in Tijuana.

Victor left Nicaragua for the same reasons that Ramon did. He works in a Tijuana factory and is making the equivalent of $25 a week. I asked Victor if he had any second thoughts about going on to

Father Rigoni talking to Ramon.

the United States. "No," he said, quite firmly. He is one of the volunteer workers helping Father Rigoni and is beginning to turn over in his mind the idea of going back to school and studying to become a priest.

Later in the afternoon, Paul told Father Rigoni that we would like to go to the soccer field. That was true, but at the same time I wasn't so sure it was a good idea. "What do you think those people will do if two gringos with camera and notebook show up?" I asked.

The soccer field.

Trails worn by nighttime illegal border crossers. Tijuana in the background.

Father Rigoni jumped up and started for the door. "Let us find out!" he said cheerfully.

What could I say in the face of such enthusiasm?

Father Rigoni drove us to Colonia Libertad, a poor section of Tijuana where border crossers can walk right onto the soccer field. We parked the car and walked down to the flat, rock-strewn area. People looked at us curiously but with no particular hostility that I could detect. Nevertheless, it was comforting to have the white-robed priest with us.

I had wondered why people would begin to assemble on the field so many hours before the border crossing would be attempted at dark. But once I was standing there, I think I understood a little better. Men sat in small groups talking quietly, exchanging information, and, I'm sure, building their confidence through talk. Some enterprising Tijuanans had set up food and drink stands on the field, just as if this were some kind of recreational area. Border crossers were bunched under the blue plastic awnings of the stands eating and drinking soft drinks and beer. In some places I saw men sitting on rocks drinking from tequila bottles, trying to pump up their nerve for the moment of crossing the border.

We tried to talk to some of the men. One man from El Salvador said that his brother had been murdered by the army. The man believed that he was also on the army's death list, so he left El Salvador. A young man from Mexico City said he was twenty-three years old and had never had a steady job. He was going to find one in California, he told us. But most of the men on the soccer field did not want to talk. It was not the time or place for interviews. They had other things on their minds.

As we left, I looked across at the hills and valleys in the United States where we had been the evening before. The footpaths worn by previous border crossers were clearly visible. In a few hours these people waiting on the soccer field would make them a little deeper.

The Hollow
of God's Hand

U.S. 94, A RURAL two-lane highway that parallels the border through most of San Diego County, is a refreshing change after the frenetic coastal freeways. We drove slowly, enjoying the golden mountains that would soon drop precipitously to the great interior basin of southern California. The mountains were hot and dry in July, but oak trees were green, and a stream that trailed beside the road here and there had a little water in it. Farms and an occasional village increased the sense of pastoral peacefulness. The barren mountains of Mexico were seldom out of sight.

Perhaps nothing can adequately prepare the traveler for his entrance into the Imperial Valley, but nature seems to try. Where San Diego and Imperial counties meet, the mountains abruptly turn into a weird jumble of huge boulders, strewn for miles in every direction as if flung by an enraged giant. With that sight impressed on my mind, the white and brown Imperial Valley desert and the sudden blasting heat into which we descended did not register fully until we had driven some distance.

At first it seems a joke that this hot, dry desert could be one of the richest, most productive agricultural areas of the world. Much of the six hundred square mile depression—which Indians of an earlier time called "the hollow of God's hand"—is below sea level. Average annual rainfall is less than two inches. For several months of the year the temperature soars well above 100 degrees. How could anything grow in this place?

And yet ground crops and tree crops do grow here. They grow year-round in profusion: lettuce, melons, tomatoes, sugar beets, cotton, strawberries, grapes, barley, dates, grapefruit. The annual value

36

of the agricultural produce of this small area is over $250 million. The land is some of the highest-priced in the country. The patchwork of fertile, verdant fields throughout this desert is the very color of money.

The answer, of course, is water, water from irrigation canals. Over a hundred years ago a government scientist insisted that this strange sunken desert could become a rich farming area. Ancient river floodings had laid down a deep alluvial soil. The fierce heat was a natural hothouse that would force plants to grow quickly; two crops a year would be easily possible. Efforts to bring irrigation water from the Colorado River sixty miles to the east began as early as 1901, and the first rugged settlers moved into the valley at that time. But it was not until the government's construction of the Boulder and Imperial dams on the Colorado River and the completion, in the early 1940s, of the All American Canal, that the Imperial Valley blossomed beyond anyone's imagination. The canal is eighty miles long and is a lifeline in the truest sense of the word.

ON OUR TRIPS Paul does the driving while I make notes. He does not mind this division of labor because it gives him total command of where we stop for lunch. Seamen from time immemorial have been guided on their journeys by the stars. Paul is guided by the golden arches that identify McDonald's restaurants. He can spot them at incredible distances, and they always bring him surely and safely to his destination. So it was this day that we had lunch at a McDonald's in El Centro, the county seat of Imperial County.

When I finished my Big Mac (I had not yet discovered the McDLT), I noticed that the man sitting at the next table had put down a copy of *The Imperial Valley Press*. I asked him if I could look at it.

"Keep it," he said, handing the paper to me.

The Imperial Valley Press was, as I had assumed, the local newspaper, and my eye fell quickly on an item that interested me. It was a list of federal court actions in El Centro, two columns of Hispanic names like Hernandez, Zavala, Santos, Alcarez, Ortiz, Cordova,

The All American Canal in California's Imperial Valley.

Flores, and Ochoa. All had been convicted of smuggling illegal aliens, using false documents, or illegal entry.

I pointed to the story and asked the man who had given me the paper if illegal aliens were a problem in Imperial County. He frowned briefly and said, "Depends on what you mean by problem."

"I mean do they cause trouble or take jobs away from county citizens?"

"They come here to work," the man said. "Just work. Those fellows have worked all their lives across the border where it's just as hot as it is here. They'll work when it's 120 degrees in the fields. Aren't many people who can do that—or will do it."

"Are they all illegals?" I asked.

The man shook his head. "Plenty of green carders," he said, using the term for aliens with a legal right to work in the United States. "But green card or not, we need them."

A Friendly David and Goliath

OUR DESTINATIONS in the Imperial Valley were the border cities of Calexico and Mexicali. From one end to the other, the border is dotted with United States and Mexican "sister" cities that share the international boundary. The sisters along the Texas-Mexico border are probably best known: El Paso-Juárez, Laredo-Nuevo Laredo, Brownsville-Matamoros. But Calexico and Mexicali are two of the most interesting, partly because of their history, partly because they seem too mismatched to be sisters. Calexico is a vigorous little city of sixteen thousand people. Mexicali is a giant with a population of eight hundred thousand. That makes Mexicali almost fifty times the size of Calexico.

"How can you be sister cities with that kind of difference?" I asked a Calexico store owner.

He thought a moment and then said, "Well, maybe not sisters

exactly. More like David and Goliath maybe. But friendly like. Real friendly."

Calexico and Mexicali both came into existence in 1900 when Imperial Land Company employees, making their first irrigation surveys, established their camp at this spot on the border. According to tradition, which seems to be factual but is hard to verify, a company press agent invented the name Calexico for the new town by combining parts of the words California and Mexico. He did the same thing for a village that sprang up on the other side of the border, putting the Mexico part first: Mexicali.

For years Mexicali was no more than a shabby border town, a place where workers from the Imperial Valley came on weekends to celebrate in the saloons and dance halls. Then things began to change, and again it was water that brought change. The Colorado River flows into Mexico; international treaty guarantees a portion of the irrigation water from the great river to the Mexicali Valley, the same geological formation as the Imperial Valley. With water, the Mexicali Valley has bloomed and become one of the great agricultural treasures of the Mexican economy. All the vegetable crops that are grown in the Imperial Valley are grown here, plus a great deal of wheat.

But why did Mexicali's population become so huge while Calexico remained a small—although healthy—city? One reason is that farming is much more mechanized in California than it is in Mexico. Thousands of families have flocked to the Mexicali area to work on the farms that surround the city. Mexicali is also the terminus of a major Mexican railroad, and it is the capital of the state of Baja California. The railroad and state government offices have added significantly to the city's growth.

Still, all of that cannot explain completely why Mexicali has fifty times more people than Calexico. I did not have a chance to ask a Mexican demographer for an explanation, but I did ask a waiter in a Mexicali restaurant. His answer probably was not far from what a demographer would have given me.

"Señor," he said, "Mexicans have big families and many babies."

40

Calexico, California. Signs in Spanish are seen more often than those in English.

FRED KNECHEL, Executive Director of the Calexico Chamber of Commerce, was our host in Calexico. As we were driving around I noticed that more store signs seemed to be in Spanish than in English, and I asked Fred about that.

"Calexico gets 80 percent or more of its business from Mexicali," Fred said. "Spanish is just as much the language of shopping here as English, maybe more. Mexican shoppers are the lifeblood of this town."

Later Fred gave me some figures that showed that 22 million pedestrians and vehicles had legally crossed the border from Mexicali into Calexico in 1984. "That's an average of sixty thousand people a day!" I said, awed by the magnitude of such a flow of people into the little city.

"More than that," Fred said. "Some of the cars are full of people. There would be a lot more shoppers if they could get through immigration. Some people wait a year for a one-day pass to cross the border from Mexicali."

Fred pointed out that not all border crossers come to Calexico to shop. Many are workers going to other parts of Imperial County. Still, the number is mind-boggling.

"QUALITY," a worker in a supermarket said to me when I asked him why people would come from Mexicali to buy food in Calexico. The clerk had just finished talking to a woman who bought a big sack of pinto beans. They had spoken in Spanish, and their conversation was clearly about the beans. "Those beans are clean, not full of little rocks and dirt like most Mexican beans," the clerk said. "And they taste better," he added, though he didn't say how or why.

But I got the same answer at other food places, sometimes directly from shoppers from Mexicali. Some of the foods they insisted were better on the U.S. side of the border were milk, sliced bread, rice, ice cream, and all kinds of frozen food.

"But food must be more expensive here," I said.

"Not necessarily," a store manager told me. "Some things are cheaper. We manufacture more efficiently and buy in large quantities."

Besides food, Mexicali shoppers in Calexico go in heavily for all kinds of electronic equipment, cosmetics, clothes, and toys. And a woman from Mexicali gave me still another reason why she and her friends shop in Calexico. "They are so nice, the people in the stores," she said. "They like to help you."

"There's more to it than shopping," Fred Knechel said when we were talking about the relationship between Calexico and Mexicali. "A lot more. We've got Spanish here, and they have a lot of English over there. Bus loads of school kids from Mexicali come over for programs, especially at Christmas. Our kids go over there. And sports. The high schools in Mexicali are playing American football now."

Looking through the Calexico city directory, I saw that the name of the mayor is Tirado; two of three councilmen are Torres and Rodriguez; the city attorney is Rivera; the treasurer, Mercado; the personnel director, Cruz; the fire chief, Zuniga; the planning director, Hinojosa; the public works director, Martinez; the recreation director, Lopez.

"It could be the directory of a town in Mexico," I said to Paul.

He glanced at it. "Not quite," he said. "Bert Johnson is building inspector."

Boom on the Border

MAQUILADORA.

We heard that word all the way from Tijuana to Brownsville. Thirty years ago the word wasn't in the Spanish language; today it is a household word throughout Mexico. *Maquiladoras* are factories or industrial plants that have been set up by U.S. firms in cities just over the border. When they began in 1966, there were only a few. Now every Mexican border city has them: Tijuana has 190, Mexicali, 80, Nogales, 50, Juárez, 170, Nuevo Laredo, 25, Reynosa, 25, Matamoros, 40. Over 750 *maquilas*, as they are usually called, are operating along the border, and another one goes into production every few days.

What is so special about these mostly U.S.-owned factories? Why does the government of Mexican President Miguel de la Madrid believe that they will save Mexico's desperately troubled economy?

The answer is simple. They bring hundreds of thousands of jobs to the job-starved country—260,000 in 1985. And they bring foreign exchange to Mexico—$1.8 billion in 1985. Oil is Mexico's greatest foreign money-maker, but *maquilas* are now second, ahead of tourism and agriculture.

The idea behind *maquiladoras* or "twin plants," as they are often called, is also simple. U.S. companies set up plants in Mexico. The Mexican government charges them no customs duty on product parts that they ship to their plants in Mexico. Workers in the Mexican plants assemble the product, and it is shipped back to the parent company in the United States. The U.S. government charges only a small "value added" duty on the assembled product. A wide range of U.S. industries have *maquiladora* twins: electronics, automotive parts, food processing, computer equipment are among the most important, but there are many others.

The *maquiladora* concept works because labor is so cheap in Mexico. A worker that costs a company $14 an hour in the United States may cost as little as $1 an hour in Mexico. A company can save from $5,000 to $15,000 on a single worker in a year. Even after a company pays the costs of setting up the *maquiladora*, shipping the material to the border, and shipping back the finished product, millions of dollars will still be saved every year because of reduced labor costs.

Maquiladoras have increased steadily since changes in Mexican import laws made them possible in 1966, and since 1982 the growth has been explosive. In the early 1980s, sharply falling oil prices brought about a devaluation of the peso. From about forty to a dollar, the peso's value fell so far that one dollar could buy over six hundred pesos. (By 1987 the exchange rate was well over twelve hundred pesos to the dollar.) Although Mexican labor had always been inexpensive compared to U.S. labor, the devaluation of the peso made it dramatically cheaper. The output of *maquilas* more than doubled between 1980 and 1985, from $2.2 billion to $5.2 billion.

ONE MORNING Fred Knechel drove us to Mexicali to look at the *maquilas*. This was our first time in Mexicali, and to me it had a different feeling from other border cities I had been in. The streets were

44

Worker in a maquiladora *that assembles computers.*

wide, well maintained, many tree-lined. There was a minimum of tourist glitz that assaults you the moment you cross into most border cities. I commented on this to Fred.

"Tourism is important here, too," he said. "But not like Tijuana or Juárez."

The *maquilas* in Mexicali employ sixteen thousand workers, another reason for the city's growing population. Some of the Mexicali *maquilas* belong to up-and-coming small companies whose names are not well known in the United States. Some belong to extremely well-known names: Hughes Aircraft, Rockwell International, Bell & Howell. A few Mexicali *maquilas* are wholly Mexican-owned or jointly owned by U.S.-Mexican companies.

Our first visit was to Ram-Kore Associates, one of the up-and-comers. I don't know what I was expecting, something like the wretched sweatshops I had seen during years of living in Asia, I guess. A greater difference would have been hard to imagine. The Ram-Kore *maquila* was air-conditioned; the lights were bright. The workers, most of them young women, had plenty of room. They carried out their tasks to piped-in Mexican music.

The co-owner and manager of the *maquila* is Brad Korer, a young American who lives in Calexico. He told me that the *maquila* works on order for a number of U.S. companies, mostly in California, assembling a variety of electrical equipment and computers, some of which have thousands of components. Ram-Kore has six supervising engineers.

"But we train all our assembly workers ourselves," he said. "Take them right off the street. And when we get them trained, they're just as good as U.S. workers."

I talked with a worker on her coffee break. She was twenty-one, she said, had been in Mexicali for two years, with Ram-Kore for a year. She was from a village two hundred miles to the south. She had come to Mexicali because there was no work in her village.

"And nothing to do in the village," she said. All the young men had gone north or to Mexico City.

She said she liked living in Mexicali; she stayed with relatives, so the cost was not so great. Her job with Ram-Kore was to hand-insert components in computer boards.

"I never thought I could do anything like that," she said, and she sounded pleased.

I think she had a right to be.

Our next stop was at Central Video in the Mexicali Industrial Park. Central Video is a joint undertaking of Bell & Howell of Chicago and Televisa, the giant Mexican multimedia corporation. This *maquila* duplicates video cassettes, packages them, and ships them all over the world. Central Video has the very latest technology, and the roomy, carefully air-conditioned plant is breathtakingly clean.

"One speck of dust can ruin a cassette," said Engineer Felix Castillo, who showed us around.

Relaxing workers at Central Video maquiladora, *Mexicali.*

The loading area, where magnetic tape is wound onto videocassettes, is considered a "clean room." Workers in this area wear special clothes and look as if they might be in a hospital operating room.

Engineer Castillo told us that Central Video has good relations with its workers. They give their employees special training but also screen several of Mexicali's technical schools for good candidates.

"Our work force is very stable," Castillo said. "Mexicali is stable, a proud, conservative city. People stay here. They live all their lives here."

And yet the salary scale for workers is about the same at Central Video as at other *maquilas*. The range is $4 to $12 a day, Castillo explained, with the average somewhere around $6. Management and a few highly skilled specialists are outside this scale. There are substantial fringe benefits for workers at Central Video: low-cost meals in the cafeteria, free transportation to the plant, free work clothes, shower facilities.

"Those things are important," said Engineer Castillo, who, in addition to his work at Central Video, teaches at a private Mexicali university.

"EVERYONE WANTS to start a *maquiladora*," Xavier Rivas, an executive in *Parque Industrial Mexicali*, said to us.

One of Rivas's responsibilities is to encourage U.S. companies to start *maquilas* in Mexicali, but he made clear that the Mexicali Industrial Commission does not want just any company. If a U.S. company is interested in coming to Mexicali, the Commission examines its financial condition and its health and safety record. If the company checks out positively, Rivas tries to convince its executives that Mexicali would be a good place for the company's across-the-border move.

"There are some disadvantages," Rivas admitted. "We have no major airport, no major city across the border. The heat can be a problem part of the year, and some people think we're too far away from the big population centers.

"But we are just three hours by truck away from Los Angeles and Phoenix, and we have good railroad connections. We have one of the lowest minimum wages."

I asked Rivas about the seemingly very low wage structure. His answer was blunt. "U.S. companies come to Mexico because they can save money on wages. We are competing with the Orient. The companies that want to build a plant out of the United States are going to do it. If they don't come to Mexico, they will go to Asia."

Rivas, a graduate of the University of Oklahoma, made a final point. "Mexico gets more than dollars when U.S. companies move here. We get a chance to learn a technology that we don't have. And we learn the production discipline of U.S. industry. In the future, that will be a big payoff of *maquilas*—maybe the biggest."

RETURNING TO Calexico, we found the U.S. border crossing as casual as it had been in other places. The immigration officer just glanced inside our car and asked if we were American citizens. We said yes, and he waved us on. I couldn't help thinking about how easy it had been for us to go into and out of Mexico and about how many people in Mexicali wait a year for a one-day pass across the border.

"It isn't fair," I said to Paul.

He didn't answer. Maybe I didn't say it. Maybe I just thought it.

That night as I made notes in my motel room, I tried to sort out my feelings about *maquiladoras*. No doubt they brought desperately needed jobs and dollars to Mexico. No doubt, also, they helped the economy of the U.S. border cities because Mexicans had more money to spend. And the more jobs in Mexico, the fewer illegal border crossers.

On the other hand, U.S. labor unions are alarmed because so many factories in the United States are closing and moving to Mexico, leaving American workers without jobs. But American industries have been moving to Hong Kong, Taiwan, the Philippines, and Korea for years seeking cheaper labor. If they are going to leave the country anyway, isn't it better for them to go to Mexico? Some of the money comes back to the United States, and the *maquilas* help a neighbor whose well-being is vital to us.

But, I asked myself, how would you like to try to support a family on $4 a day? Or $6 a day? Sure, things are cheaper in Mexico, but not that much cheaper. Most Mexican families had to be living on the edge of financial despair. The American economic system is built on profit-making, but couldn't U.S. corporations pay better wages in foreign countries and still make a decent profit?

And, I asked myself again, were all *maquilas* as comfort-conscious and pleasant to work in as the ones we had seen today? The answer was no. Probably almost all *maquilas* are better than their Asian equivalents. But there still are *maquilas* where employees work in crowded, poorly ventilated buildings that are fire hazards, where the lighting is poor and safety precautions are nil. We hadn't seen any *maquilas* that fitted that description, but I had heard about them and read about them. They were there.

There was one more thing. Xavier Rivas had said that the Mexicali Industrial Commission checks the health and safety records of companies that want to start *maquilas*. But it is well known that some Mexicali *maquilas* are dumping toxic industrial waste into the New River that flows into California. This waste causes great damage to plant and animal life, not only in the river but also in the Salton Sea, a great Imperial Valley lake into which the river empties.

I read over my notes. They went around in a circle, just the way my head was going. I turned on the TV and watched an old John Wayne movie.

The Desert
of Death

I WAS THINKING about John Wayne the next day when we crossed the Colorado River and drove into Yuma, where Arizona, California, and Mexico meet. Here is the confluence of the Colorado and Gila rivers, and here, in desert and mountains, is the pure stuff of Western history. Yuma Crossing was the destination of thousands of California-bound pioneers and gold seekers after the Mexican War. Fort Yuma, built on the west bank of the Colorado in 1852, protected the emigrants and kept peace between local settlers and Indians. Stories of gold so plentiful that Indians used gold bullets in their guns caused a gold rush to this part of Arizona in the 1850s.

Gold was in the river, but the real gold was the river itself. Irrigation of arid desert began in the early 1900s; today almost three hundred thousand acres of farms and orchards have made Yuma a major center of agriculture. Yuma County produces 75 percent of all citrus grown in Arizona.

Prison Hill is a good place to get a sense of the past in this dramatic coming together of desert, mountains, and rivers. The old

The old Territorial Prison, Yuma, Arizona.

At Territorial Prison in Arizona.

Territorial Prison was established in 1876 on a granite bluff that overlooks river and city. Only the cells, the dungeon, dug from solid rock, the main gate, and the guard tower remain as grim reminders of the harshness of frontier justice. Prisoners thinking about escaping could look out and see nothing but waterless desert and stark mountains for hundreds of miles in every direction. But the terrible heat of summer and the unbroken loneliness were such that many prisoners tried to escape. A few succeeded. Some died in the desert. Most were caught by Indians, who were paid $50 for every escapee they brought back to the prison.

Paul and I were at the ruins on a blazing July afternoon, and I understood why the inmates' name for the prison had been the "hell hole." Although the prison is now a state park, no one was there in the midday heat except us. Just as we were leaving, an old man came in and sat down against the adobe wall of a building. He seemed to belong to a page of Territorial history, an apparition from the past.

Paul asked the man if he could take his picture for a book. "Don't see why you want it," the man said, "but go ahead."

For twenty-three miles the southward-flowing Colorado River forms the international boundary between Arizona and Baja California. Except for this, the border cuts its way eastward through the desert, separating Arizona from the Mexican state of Sonora. East of Yuma the desert assumes its most severe form. There is no water. The crusty, alkaline flats are shadeless. Miles of sand dunes, almost impossible to walk through, rise up out of the flats. Temperatures reach 120 degrees during the summer months. A few animals have learned to live in this place, but rattlesnakes and scorpions are most at home here.

The desert of death the area is sometimes called and with good reason. In the past five years the bodies or bones of more than sixty illegal aliens, in more than one case families including small children, have been found half buried in the sand or pitifully curled under some stunted mesquite or greasewood bush. How many bodies lie undiscovered in the desert no one can guess.

The desert of death.

We talked to Deputy Chief Border Patrol Agent Johnny Williams at the Yuma Sector headquarters. "East of here is the most dangerous part of the border," he said. "Illegals have to cross thirty to sixty miles of desert and mountains before they reach any orchards or farms where they can get water.

"Some lose their way and just wander around until they die. They don't take enough water. They can't carry enough, especially in cases of families with children."

"Why do they try to cross that desert when there are so many other places to get across the border?" I asked. "Places a lot easier and less dangerous."

"Some of them don't know how dangerous it is," Johnny Williams said. "They think it's just a little walk. Some know its dangerous but think their chances of not getting caught are better if they go across the desert."

"Are their chances better?"

"Some get through," Johnny said, "but we catch plenty. This part of the border is more enforceable than some other parts."

I thought about the thousands of illegals pouring across the border in San Diego County, and I understood what he meant.

"But why do they cross the desert in the summer, when it's like a blast furnace out there?" I asked.

"The height of the citrus-picking season is August and September," Johnny said. "They come when the jobs are there. Illegals from Central America just cross any time they get here."

Border Patrol Agent J. H. (Joe) McCraw works out of the Tacna Station, one of three Border Patrol stations in the Yuma Sector, which covers 28,150 square miles. Tacna is in the desert forty miles east of Yuma and near the rugged Mohawk Mountains, through which illegals sometimes come in a further effort to avoid being caught. A few miles east of Tacna is Dateland, where irrigated citrus orchards are a prime destination of illegals. Joe McCraw has spent ten of his seventeen years as an agent in this area, and he has become one of the Border Patrol's best and most experienced trackers.

"Cutting sign, it used to be called out here in the West," Joe told us. "Trailing a man by the signs he leaves behind him as he walks—

Cutting sign. Border Patrol Agent J. H. McCraw in the desert near Tacna Station east of Yuma.

footprints mainly, but sign might be a cigarette butt, an empty to-mato can, a broken branch on a bush, a mashed down place where he slept or rested. Things like that. When we're out on patrol and come across sign, we follow it if it's fresh enough. Chances are the sign will lead us to our man."

"How do you tell a fresh print from an old one?" I asked.

"Come on," Joe said. "I'll show you."

We drove a short way into the desert on one of the Border Patrol drag roads that are maintained for better coverage of the area. Soon we stopped, got out, and walked down the road. It wasn't long before Joe found some footprints.

"Illegals head for the roads," he said. "Like to walk down them at night. That's fine with us. Prints on the road are easy to spot."

Joe stepped carefully beside one of the footprints, leaving his own print pressed clearly in the dust. "Look at the difference," he said. "That other print is maybe two days old. It's faint. The wind has rounded off the edges. See how much deeper and sharper my print is. That's the print to follow. If I followed the other one, I'd have a long walk for nothing."

Joe took us out into the desert. "An illegal will try a lot of tricks to throw off a tracker," he said. He pulled a branch from a mesquite bush and used it to brush out some of his own tracks.

"Brushin' out," he said. "They'll do that sometimes when their tracks are too plain."

Joe walked backward for a short distance, planting his feet firmly so that his tracks were clear. "Sometimes they'll walk backward," he said, "maybe when they're walking through a wash or a dry stream bed. Been a long time since I've been fooled by that."

"I've heard there aren't many good trackers," I said to Joe, "that it's almost a lost art. What would you say is the main thing that makes a good tracker?"

Joe thought for a minute. "Patience, I guess," he said. "If you lose the sign, you keep looking until you pick it up again. You don't get discouraged. And you learn to look for something different, something that isn't quite right. You ask yourself what you would do if you were trying to keep a tracker off your trail. And then you do just what you think that fellow did."

Joe talked about the tragic cases of illegal border crossers lost in the desert. "We're always looking for their sign," he said, "and we try our best to find them before they die."

"What sign tells you someone is lost?" I asked.

"You'll see a footmark that's beginning to drag," Joe said.

"Tracks that are beginning to zigzag. You'll see signs that a bag is being dragged or that someone is sitting down or falling down. Maybe you'll find a discarded bag or clothes. If we're lucky—if they're lucky—we'll find them before it's too late.

"Sometimes an illegal will come stumbling into the Border Patrol office and tell us that a friend or maybe a whole group is out in the desert, dying. They're out of water and they can't go any farther. They're just waiting to die. Usually the fellow doesn't have much of an idea where he's been. He's probably delirious, but we get all the information we can out of him, and then we call in DART— that's the Desert Area Rescue Team. We have several rescue teams, all volunteers, all good trackers. As part of their training, they've been flown over the area they cover until they have a good idea of the whole terrain. When the team goes out, they have extra water, first-aid gear, and trucks equipped with floodlights for night work. We get a plane in on the search when we can. Those pilots are good trackers, too."

"Do you always find them?" I asked.

"If we cut their sign, we find them," Joe said. "Most of them are still alive." He stared out into the desert. "But not always."

The League of Desperate Men

"THESE MEN slept on the ground," Lupe Sanchez said. "They stretched a piece of plastic between two trees in the orchard and slept under it. Some of them didn't have money to buy a piece of plastic. They didn't have blankets. They didn't have drinking water except from the irrigation ditches."

We were in the town of El Mirage near Phoenix talking to Lupe Sanchez, Executive Director of the Arizona Farmworkers Union. We were talking about the undocumented workers (you do not use the term "illegal aliens" in Lupe's presence) who come from Mexico every year to harvest lemons, grapefruit, and oranges in the area around El Mirage. This was the only time we left the border zone in our entire journey, but we knew that the story of Lupe and the coura-geous men he represents belonged in a book about the border.

"The orchard owners didn't care," Lupe said. "They wanted

Lupe Sanchez.

their citrus picked the cheapest way. They paid the smallest hourly wages they could. They gave nothing to help the men live. Who could the men complain to? They weren't supposed to be here. They had crossed the border without papers. If they complained about their treatment, Immigration would just send them back to Mexico.

"This was in 1976. It had been like this for years, and it wasn't getting any better. Maybe it was worse. We had to do something."

Lupe could use the word "we" even though he was not a migrant farmworker in 1976. Born in Monterrey, Mexico, he was ten years old when his family immigrated to McAllen, Texas, in 1955. Lupe's family traveled over much of the United States as farm laborers.

"Michigan, Ohio, Indiana, California, Oregon, Texas, of course," he told us. "We harvested ground crops and tree crops." Lupe smiled and added, "In 1960 we ran out of money in Arizona and just stayed here."

Lupe studied in night school, became a U.S. citizen, worked as an organizer for the United Farmworkers Union. He received special training in California, where, under Cesar Chavez, that union gained considerable strength. Lupe became increasingly well known to farmworkers around El Mirage and was trusted by them. In 1975, the El Mirage city council appointed Lupe Sanchez as the presiding city magistrate. He became Judge Sanchez.

But from that position he could see even more clearly the desperate plight of undocumented workers who had no protection and no voice to speak for them. Less than two years after becoming city magistrate, Lupe resigned to help the undocumented workers from Mexico find their voice. Lupe knew labor organizing, but the idea of a union of undocumented workers—people with no legal standing in the country—seemed out of the question. The idea of their going on strike seemed even more absurd.

"But," said Lupe, "what other hope was there?"

And so, during the latter part of 1976 and the first part of 1977, the groundwork for the first organization of undocumented workers, the Arizona Farmworkers Union, was laid. And, should it be necessary, plans for the first strike by undocumented workers were made. This groundwork was carried out by Lupe and a few determined un-

Members of the Arizona Farmworkers Union.

documented workers. They had advice and help from civil rights lawyers and especially from a hard-hitting investigative reporter named Don Devereux, who is even now volunteer press secretary for the union.

"We sent a committee of workers back to Mexico to recruit and organize for the next harvest season," Lupe said. "We met with workers in six Mexican states who knew they were coming to Arizona, and we organized strike committees in all those places. We told the workers to come prepared for a strike and for a hard time. We had a little money from dues and from contributions by people who believed in what we were doing. That summer of 1977 we slipped into the citrus ranches and buried canned food in many places so that if a strike was necessary the workers could not be starved out."

In August the workers returned, many crossing the desert on foot, and made their way to El Mirage. That month the young union presented the corporate citrus orchards around Phoenix with a list of demands. They wanted to be paid the legal minimum wage. They wanted a blanket for each worker. They wanted a piece of plastic for each worker. They wanted clean drinking water and toilets in the orchards. They wanted no trees sprayed with insecticide while men were working in them.

The orchard owners refused these demands, and on October 3 the first strike of undocumented workers in U.S. history began. "I think they could not believe it at first," Lupe said. "The owners could not believe that something like that could happen. And then after two days and no fruit was being picked they believed it, and they went crazy.

"They tried to frighten us. They had the Border Patrol arrest some of the men and take them to the border at Nogales. But the men just came back. The men were just sitting under the trees, waiting. The sheriff and his deputies tried to arrest them, but the men moved to other places in the orchard. And then the owners thought, 'If we get rid of these men, who will pick the fruit?' They went to 'coyotes' and said, 'Bring us new workers.' But we knew all the 'coyotes' and everything they had done. We said to them, 'If you bring in new men,

The citrus pickers don't have to sleep under the trees now, but their quarters still leave much to be desired.

we will report you to Immigration and testify against you.' The 'coyotes' disappeared. They just vanished, and the growers had no way to get new workers."

Now it was the growers who were desperate. Their fruit had to be picked or they faced financial ruin. After ten days twenty citrus ranches waved the white flag and agreed to all the workers' demands. The strike was over.

Today the Arizona Farmworkers Union has between fifteen and twenty thousand active members. There is a great turnover of workers, but the union is strong. "A worker is a worker," Lupe said. "What does it matter whether he was born in Mexico or in the United States?"

Wages for workers have quadrupled in the past six years, and long-term contracts for workers have been signed between the union and a number of orchard owners. Thinking of those early days when there was nothing but raw courage and a sense of justice to sustain them, Lupe said: "A decent wage, a blanket, some clean water to drink, the right not to be sprayed with insecticide—I do not think that was too much to ask."

The Sun Seekers

TUCSON, 125 miles east of Phoenix, is one of the fastest-growing cities in the border zone. In 1940 its population was about forty thousand, and it was a cozy little city whose traditional name, The Old Pueblo, seemed appropriate. Today Tucson sprawls over ninety-seven square miles of high desert valley and is home to four hundred thousand people. Far from its growth tapering off, an estimated two thousand new permanent residents arrive every month. The number of illegal residents is not known, but informed estimates run high.

Fortunately, growth cannot diminish the loveliness of Tucson's location. In every direction are mountains of rugged beauty: the Santa Catalinas to the north, Santa Ritas to the south, Rincons to the east, Tucsons to the west. Indian, Mexican, and Anglo cultures have mingled in this desert setting for a long time. First this was Indian land, and the name Tucson itself derives from ancient Indian words, *Chuk Shon*, which meant "spring at the base of black mountain." Three Yaqui Indian villages thrive within the metropolitan Tucson area, and their Lenten and Holy Week ceremonies add color to the city. The Yaquis fled from Mexico around the end of the nineteenth century to escape oppression by the Mexican government. They are not considered a U.S. tribe by the Bureau of Indian Affairs, but they are certainly permanent residents. The Tohono O'odham Indian reservation a few miles west of Tucson is the second largest in the United States.

Mission San Xavier del Bac, White Dove of the Desert.

Mexican roots in Tucson go back for centuries, and it was a Mexican town until the Gadsden Purchase in 1853. Mission San Xavier del Bac, thirteen miles southwest of Tucson, was built by a Franciscan father between 1783 and 1797. Called the White Dove of the Desert, it is one of the finest examples of Spanish mission architecture. *Cinco de Mayo*, a four-day festival, is Tucson's biggest and most popular public event; it celebrates the victory of Mexican soldiers over French troops on May 5, 1862. A statue of Mexican folk hero Pancho Villa occupies a prominent place in a downtown Tucson park.

In addition to its scenic and ethnic richness, Tucson is one of only fourteen cities in the United States that have a professional symphony orchestra, a professional resident theater, and opera and dance companies. It is also the home of the University of Arizona.

Statue of Pancho Villa in downtown Tucson.

Do all these attractions explain Tucson's mushrooming growth since 1940? They have contributed to it, but the major reason is to be found in something else: the sun. Tucson has an average of 360 days of sunshine a year. Summers are blazing hot, but winters are delightful; rain is scarce, and the rare snowfall is seldom more than a dusting. Swimming, golf, tennis, horseback riding, and every other outdoor activity are possible almost every day from November through March.

Since the 1960s a steady internal migration in the United States from the "snowbelt" to the "sunbelt" has been underway. While no standard definition of the sunbelt exists, it is generally understood to include all states of the "Confederate South" plus Oklahoma, New Mexico, Arizona, and California. The entire U.S.-Mexican border zone is thus included in this definition.

Because of climate and opportunities for a more leisurely and informal lifestyle, many older Americans have moved to the sunbelt, with Florida, California, and Arizona their favorite destinations. In the border zone, not only Tucson but every other major city and some smaller cities and towns, such as Del Rio, Texas, and Deming, New Mexico, have had population increases because of migration of older Americans from the northern part of the country.

But migration to the sunbelt border zone is not limited to older people. For the past twenty years, important segments of U.S. industry have moved south and brought ambitious young people with them. These industries include high technology such as electronics, aerospace, and energy and service industries such as real estate, tourism, and recreation. Among the most important reasons for the geographic shift of these industries are lower energy costs, labor supply, an excellent highway network, and major air terminals unhampered by bad weather.

Tourism booms in the border zone during the winter months. Hundreds of thousands of northerners arrive, many for long stays. Tucson is surrounded by dude ranches, almost all fully booked throughout the season. "Snowbirds," as northerners escaping bad weather are called, double Yuma's population from fifty thousand to one hundred thousand every winter. Yuma is surrounded by forty-

Helen Brunk and her husband moved to Yuma when they retired. They manage a motel for a few months a year and "play" the rest of the time.

seven trailer parks. "Winter Texans" are an important part of the border economy from El Paso to Brownsville.

For job-hungry Mexicans across the border, the new sunbelt industries, the snowbirds, the well-to-do retired senior citizens mean work opportunities. Besides factory and construction work, the possibilities for service jobs in restaurants, hotels, motels, fast-food chains, and recreational facilities are huge.

At our motel in Tucson, I talked to a young Mexican woman who had been working there as a maid for six months. She said she was always looking over her shoulder for fear of the Border Patrol. "Why?" she asked. "Why do they want to send me back? Who wants this job but me?"

About 25 percent of Tucson's four hundred thousand people are Mexican-Americans or legal Mexican aliens. We talked to Francisco Hoyos, immigration counselor for Catholic Social Services, and got some hard facts about the chances of immigrating legally from Mexico to the United States.

"When I came to Tucson in 1954," Mr. Hoyos said, "all a person had to do to have legal resident status was show INS evidence that you had a job. I had a job in a flower nursery, so I became a legal alien."

Hoyos stayed in Tucson and became a U.S. citizen. "But today," he said, "the road to legal status is very hard. Having a job does not count anymore unless it can be proved that no American citizen is available to fill the job. How can you prove that?

"About the only way to get in legally today is family reunification. But even naturalized American citizens have long waits to bring in spouses and children, even longer for brothers and sisters and parents. The wives and children of legal aliens in the United States may have to wait eight years for a visa to come here. I work every day with these people who want to legally bring their family members in Mexico here to live with them."

"How many U.S. visas for Mexicans a year?" I asked. "Twenty thousand?"

"For the whole United States," Hoyos exclaimed. "We could use all of them right here in Tucson!"

The Thirst-Enduring People

WEST OF TUCSON, the Tohono O'odham Indian reservation stretches along the Mexican border for sixty miles and covers a chunk of the Arizona Sonoran Desert the size of Connecticut. It is the only Indian reservation in the four border states that shares the international boundary with Mexico.

The Tohono O'odham (pronounced to-HONE-no AH-tomb)

were the first Indians encountered in this area by the sixteenth-century Spanish explorers. The Spaniards called them Papago (Bean Eaters), and to this day they are known as the Papago tribe by almost everyone. But their ancient tribal name in their own language was Tohono O'odham, and that is what they call themselves. Some say the name means the Desert People; some say it means the Thirst-Enduring People. Either meaning seems to fit in this land of little rain. It is said that long ago O'odham fathers would awaken their children in the morning by whispering, "Drink very little water today."

About eight thousand O'odham live on their desert reservation. They eke out a living by dry farming, raising a few cattle, weaving baskets, and finding occasional jobs. Many O'odham live in villages that have no electricity, no running water, no telephones. Some do not have cars. Most O'odham, even the children, still speak the tribal language, although most speak English also.

Life is easier for the two thousand O'odham who live in the tribal headquarters town of Sells. Sells is a modern community with some good federal housing, comfortable tribal offices, elementary school, health clinic, and churches. The Bureau of Indian Affairs has an office here. The tribe and the BIA are the biggest employers on the reservation, hiring teachers, office workers, nurses, laborers, and social service workers. But the unemployment rate on the reservation is still one of the highest in the nation, and the income level one of the lowest.

Josiah Moore, the tribal chairman, is a visionary man who wants to bring more schools, more roads, more economic opportunity to the reservation. He wants the O'odham to retain their tribal traditions, but he knows that poverty is driving people off the reservation.

"Some may say that progress brings problems," Moore said, "but there sure are problems now."

One morning we stood deep inside the reservation with Leatrice Wilson, a member of the O'odham tribe, looking at a tragic reminder of one grim problem now deeply troubling these desert border people. We were at the grave of Glenn Miles, a veteran Customs Service patrol officer who was also a member of the O'odham tribe.

Leatrice Wilson at the grave of Customs Service Agent Glenn Miles.

On a February night in 1985, Miles was murdered on this spot while trying to intercept three drug smugglers.

Miles was born and raised on the O'odham reservation. He had been in law enforcement for sixteen years, five as a member of the tribal police force and eleven as a Customs Service patrol officer, a job he loved. He was an experienced tracker, and he knew the desert as well as any man. Yet on that ill-fated night, he apparently walked into an ambush; he was shot several times with two guns, one of them his own.

Marijuana and cocaine smugglers from Mexico for years have used the isolated O'odham reservation as a major route for entering the United States. Most of the cocaine is brought in at night by low-flying airplanes that land at unmarked desert strips or drop their contraband at places where accomplices are waiting.

Marijuana, however, is backpacked through the reservation by men who are paid from $200 to $300 for a trip from across the border to some agreed-upon place outside the reservation. Their loads range from fifty to one hundred pounds. After the marijuana is delivered, it is taken to a "stash house" in Tucson and later sent all over the United States. Travis Kuykendall, head of the Drug Enforcement Administration in Tucson, reports that most of the thirteen thousand tons of marijuana grown in Mexico every year are brought to the United States through Arizona.

Intercepting drug smugglers is a dangerous business everywhere but probably nowhere more dangerous than in the lonely Sonoran Desert. Customs Service patrol agents work in teams; but on the night Miles was killed, his two partners were working in one car and he was alone in another so that they could cover more territory. About 9:30 Miles radioed that he had spotted three backpackers heading north from the border. He said he was going to follow them on foot, and he asked his partners to back him up.

When they found him half an hour later, Miles was dead. His murderers have not yet been caught despite a massive and still ongoing investigation. The Customs Service has offered a $100,000 reward for information leading to the arrest and conviction of the killers, but no one has come forward to try to claim the reward. Evidence gathered indicates that the killers were from Mexico; but even if anyone living on the O'odham reservation knew anything, they might be afraid to talk.

"Yes, afraid," an O'odham tribal member said. "A hundred thousand dollars is a lot of money, but not enough to die for. They might kill you for talking."

"They" is a vague word and was meant to be vague. The murder of Glenn Miles has sent shock waves through the O'odham reservation. A general belief exists that some tribal members are involved in drug smuggling. An official of the tribe has said he is sure that some people on the reservation are being "paid off" for cooperating with smugglers. Giving illegal border crossers a ride to Tucson or Phoenix for a price is fairly common, and it is a law violation that has caused some O'odham to have their cars confiscated.

When people are as poor as the Tohono O'odham and the temptation of easy drug- and alien-smuggling money is so great, some will yield to that temptation. But the idea that some member of Miles' own tribe may have been involved in his death is a possibility that no O'odham will voice.

When we left Glenn Miles's grave, Leatrice drove us to the border, only a few miles away. The road is a two-lane blacktop that cuts a straight line through the starkly beautiful Sonoran Desert vegetation. Rainy season clouds built up overhead, but Baboquivari Peak, sacred mountain of the O'odham tribe, stood out clearly in the east. We had not met a single car since we left Sells, and we did not meet one on the way back. It is hard to believe that such roads still exist in America.

And then we were at the barbed-wire fence that marks the border between the United States and Mexico. A cattle guard is built into the road so that cattle cannot stray into or out of Mexico, but there is no gate and no customs or immigration officials are on duty on either side. Cattle can't go from one country to the other, but people can, with no control at all. The blacktop becomes a dirt road in Mexico. I could see no other change.

The Tohono O'odham in Mexico do much of their living in the outdoor ramada.

"If I were going to sneak from Mexico into the United States, I would do it right here," I said.

"Lots of people do," Leatrice said, "and lots of them get picked up by the Border Patrol before they are out of the reservation." She pointed to four young Mexicans sitting under a palo verde tree. "They're waiting for dark to cross," she said. "If the Border Patrol watched this crossing, they would just climb over the fence some-place else."

In 1853 the Gadsden Purchase changed the U.S.-Mexican border so that it cut directly through land on which the O'odham tribe had lived for centuries. The new border left two-thirds of the tribe on the U.S. side and one-third on the Mexican side. Over the years many of those in Mexico have moved to the reservation in the United States, but hundreds have continued to live in villages on the Mexican side of the border.

Leatrice Wilson was born in Mexico. She spent her childhood years in the village of Pozo Verde, a tiny O'odham community with no electricity, no telephones, no school or stores, just a few families living side by side. Leatrice remembers those years as the best of her life.

"We were poor, but so was everyone else," she told us. "My father raised some cattle and horses. There were kids to play with, and we were like one big family. At Christmas we would all go to the church a few miles away and have a feast and watch Christmas plays."

Now Leatrice lives in Sells and is in charge of a tribal program called The O'odham in Mexico. The purpose of the program is to keep a census count of the O'odham across the border and to help them establish title to their land in Mexico.

We drove a few miles into Mexico and met some of the O'odham tribe who live there. They are older people almost entirely. Families with young children have moved to the reservation because of the school, but occasionally someone moves back from the reser-vation to live in Mexico. The border has never had any real meaning

Ramon Noriego, a member of the Tohono O'odham tribe living in Mexico.

for the O'odham. It is a line that separates countries, but it cannot separate a tribe.

As we drove back to Sells, I thought about the centuries of pressures that this little tribe has withstood: first their ancient enemies, the Apaches; then the Spaniards; then the Americans. Now the drug smugglers, who may be the most dangerous of all. Will the Thirst-Enduring People endure? I think they will.

Two Lively Cities and a Town Too Tough to Die

I KNEW THE MAYOR of Nogales, Arizona, was going to be a nice guy. I called him at his home on a Sunday, got him out of a shower after a softball game, and he was still cheerful and polite when he agreed to see us in his office the next day. I usually don't call mayors, or anyone else, at home on Sunday to talk business, but timing was critical in our travels, and we didn't want to miss Nogales—either one of them.

Ambos Nogales means "Nogales together" or "both Nogales," and we had heard that is the way city officials and most residents think about their twin border cities—one city separated by a fence. An *Ambos Nogales* Commission with eight city officers from Nogales, Sonora, and eight from Nogales, Arizona, meet regularly to talk about joint projects and solve joint problems. Over 85 percent of the people in the U.S. Nogales speak Spanish. Hundreds of children from Nogales, Sonora, cross the border to go to school, and one reason is that their parents want them to learn to speak English fluently. But some Mexican-American parents in Nogales, Arizona, send their sons and daughters to schools in Nogales, Sonora, because they want them to have both languages and not lose their Mexican heritage.

"In many ways we are like one city," Mayor Marcelino Varona, Jr., told us when we met, "maybe like one big family. So many families have relatives on both sides of the border. I think the two Nogales are closer than any of the other border twin cities."

I was right in my hunch: Mayor Varona is a very nice guy. He is also a forceful, energetic administrator who dealt with the questions and problems of a steady stream of his city hall staff while we were talking with him. I was astonished to learn that, in addition to his civic duties, the mayor is assistant principal at Nogales High School and runs a family-owned flower store. He is also finishing work on a Ph.D. degree in education at the University of Arizona.

"Isn't being mayor a full-time job?" I asked.

Mayor Varona smiled. "I think so," he said, "but the salary is fifty dollars a month."

It is true that, with a population of seventeen thousand, Nogales, Arizona, is not a big city; but having a sister city of 180,000 on its doorstep creates complexities that much larger cities away from the border do not have. "What is their problem," the mayor said, speaking of Nogales, Sonora, "eventually becomes our problem.

"Take dogs, a simple thing like that. We have very strict laws about vaccinating dogs against rabies. Not so strict over there and hard to enforce. But how can we keep Mexican dogs from coming into the United States? There are holes in the border fence. And they don't stop for immigration check when they want to come over. So we have to try to help with their rabies program.

"And take something much bigger," Mayor Varona continued. "From 70 to 90 percent of Nogales, Sonora, sewage is treated right here in our plant because we have the capacity and they don't. They fell behind on their payment for this service. We tried to get a federal subsidy to help. Some people said, 'Why don't you just block the line and cut the service? Let the sewage stay in Mexico.' But is the border fence going to keep the disease from spreading to my city? I don't think so. Besides, that isn't the thing to do.

"Our fire departments help each other and so do our police departments. We go over there and learn about their system, and they learn about ours. And maybe relatives are working in the police and fire departments in both cities. That helps."

Mayor Marcelino Varona.

The fifty *maquiladoras* in Nogales, Sonora, provide a great part of that city's income, and the spillover to Nogales, Arizona, is great. I recalled a Senate International Trade Commission study that showed 40 to 60 percent of all wages earned in *maquilas* are spent in stores and shops in the United States. The study also reported the surprising fact that 50 percent of the money spent by Mexicans in Arizona in 1984 was spent in Nogales.

"I need for those people to come over here and spend money," the mayor said. "This town has no property tax. We depend on a 1 percent sales tax for our city income. If shoppers stopped coming across the border, we'd be in big trouble.

"I'll tell you how close we're linked. The economic health of my town depends more on what the Mexican President and his finance minister do than on President Reagan and the secretary of the treasury."

We had heard a good deal about Cesar Dabdoub Chavez, the *presidente municipal*—mayor—of Nogales, Sonora; unfortunately, we could not meet him on this trip because he was out of the city. Mayor Dabdoub's father was a Palestinian who came to Mexico from Bethlehem in 1903. The Dabdoub family became very prominent, both financially and politically, in Sonora. Mayor Dabdoub has sent his children to schools in the United States. When criticized for this, he replies that as children of the border, they need to know both languages and both cultures.

"The most interesting part of my job," said Mayor Varona, "is dealing with a mayor in a foreign country. The system is different— in Mexico you are guilty until proven innocent! The pressures are different. Every time I meet with Mayor Dabdoub I learn something new about Mexico.

"There is something all the time. Once the police in our city were making trouble for taxi drivers from over there, so their police started making trouble for our taxi drivers when they took passengers across the border. Mayor Dabdoub and I met and talked things over and settled the problem with a handshake. Sometimes I need something and will call the mayor. Sometimes he will call me and say something like, 'Hey, I need three dump trucks today,' and I will send them. We get along and help each other, and that sends a message to everyone."

When we left, I couldn't resist asking, "What about the future? Are you going to be an educator or a politician?"

"I don't know," Mayor Varona said. "When I have time, I have to think about that."

To THE EAST of Nogales is Cochise County, which fairly drips Western history. The county is named for Cochise, the Chiricahua Apache chief who led his tribe in a bitter but hopeless struggle against the U.S. Army in the latter half of the nineteenth century. The border played a part in the struggle; when army pressure became too great, the Apache would slip into Mexico where the troops were forbidden to follow.

Fort Huachuca, from which the U.S. Cavalry campaigned against the Apache, is still in operation, the oldest active army base in the United States. But most visitors to Cochise County head for Tombstone, which proudly bills itself as "the town too tough to die." History records that Tombstone was a rough, tough silver-mining town between 1879 and 1890, when underground water made the mines unprofitable. But a small, determined population continued to live there, and the town's famous landmarks have been preserved as a National Historic Site: The Bird Cage Theatre, the Crystal Palace Saloon, the Wells Fargo Office, Boothill Cemetery, and a good deal more.

To moviegoers and television watchers, Tombstone probably is best remembered as the place where Marshal Wyatt Earp, his brother Virgil, and Doc Holliday had their famous gunfight with the Clanton and McLaury brothers at the O.K. Corral. The O.K. Corral is still there and, for a dollar, the visitor to Tombstone can see where the battle was fought.

We stopped in Tombstone because we wanted to meet Roy McNeely, who is the present marshal of the little town. Born in West Virginia, McNeely has spent most of his forty-two years driving trucks, singing and playing guitar in country music bands, and work-

Roy McNeely, the Marshal of Tombstone.

ing in law enforcement. He has been marshal of Tombstone since 1984, but he moonlights with his own little country music group called Roy Mac and the Tombstone Desperadoes.

Tombstone isn't the lawman's challenge that it was in the days of men like Wyatt Earp and Sheriff John Slaughter. Today the board sidewalks are filled with tourists in shorts and floppy hats, not tough miners, tinhorn gamblers, and gun-toting outlaws. Even so, McNeely carries out his duties as marshal with a seriousness that disturbs many of Tombstone's seventeen hundred permanent residents. They say that he has the fastest draw in the West in reaching for his parking-ticket book. They say he treats running a stop sign like a federal crime, and they can't see why he has to arrest someone who gets a bit boisterous after spending too much time in the Crystal Palace.

Marshal McNeely looks at it differently. "This town belongs to the people of America," he told us. "As long as I'm marshal, it's going to be a place tourists can enjoy and feel safe in."

Tombstone is just twenty miles from the border, and marijuana can find its way easily into the town. "But anybody smoking it had better watch out," the marshal said. "I can smell it a mile away."

When we left, McNeely gave me a cassette of Roy Mac and the Tombstone Desperadoes. I am not a connoisseur of country music, but when I played the tape I liked it, partly I think because the marshal puts himself into a song just as he does into enforcing the law.

Maybe the good citizens of Tombstone think their marshal takes himself too seriously, but I believe I know how Roy McNeely feels. When you pin on a marshal's badge and walk the same streets that Wyatt Earp, Bat Masterson, and John Slaughter walked, you are a part of history. That is serious business.

"It's a Great Big Gamble"

RANCHING IS THE HEART and blood of the border country. *Maquiladoras* are important in the border cities. In places where irrigation brings abundant water, like the Imperial Valley of California and the lower Rio Grande Valley of Texas, vegetables and citrus are big money-makers. But for most of its two thousand miles the border cuts through parched land that would be worthless except for cattle.

Joe Bill Nunn is a rancher in Luna County, New Mexico, one of the border counties. "This grass and these weeds would be worth nothing if we didn't convert them to beef," he said. "The forage is a renewable resource because we use it and take care of it."

At sunup we waited on the edge of the prairie for Joe Bill and his crew to drive steers in from a holding pen to the shipping corral. The sun rises over the Goodsight Hills east of the Nunn ranch. One minute darkness is everywhere; the next minute, light floods the prairie and turns the grass into a sea of gold.

With the light came the yearlings, raising great clouds of dust and bawling nonstop as they were herded into the corral by Joe Bill and the other riders. Once there, the cattle were driven in bunches of seventeen onto a scale; each bunch weighed close to fourteen thousand pounds. After the weigh-in each steer was examined by an inspector from the New Mexico Livestock Board. He checks to see that each animal carries one of the Nunn family brands; both Joe Bill and his father, Ed, were shipping cattle. After the inspection the cattle were driven into huge double-decker trucks to begin the nine-hour ride to the feeding lots in Lubbock, Texas. They would stay there for 130 to 150 days, putting on another three to four hundred pounds each. Then they would go to slaughter houses in different parts of the country.

Two hundred steers sold for $100,000 that morning. Joe Bill figured that at least $90,000 of that had already been invested in this herd, leaving maybe $10,000 profit. The Nunns held out three hundred steers for later shipment with the hope that in a month the market would be a few cents a pound better. But during that time there might be a snow—this was mid-November—and their cattle could lose fifty to a hundred pounds each in just a few days. Plenty of times they have lost similar gambles.

"It is heartbreaking to see a load of cattle go down the road and you know that you have lost money on them," Joe Bill said.

But today he was elated. "This was a big kick, and it will keep us going for a long time. We can take this money to the bank and pay on our note."

A rancher pays on his ranch all his life and, if he is lucky and a good manager, may finally get out of debt when he is sixty-five. That, at least, is the rule of thumb of Smokey Nunn (who prefers that name to Ed).

"I'm still buying the ranch," Smokey told us. "I've been doing it for years. Every winter after I ship my last cattle I go in and borrow more money. I'm never out of debt." And then he added, "Ranching is a great big gamble. That's the only way I can describe it."

The problem, Joe Bill explains, is that the profit margin is so small and so many things affect that margin. The price of beef may drop suddenly; the rancher really is at the mercy of the market. The "seemingly unlimited" number of cattle that come out of Mexico affect price and make it hard for the American rancher to plan. Cattle can die from diseases like leptospirosis and pneumonia and from eating poison weeds. Predators, mostly coyotes but sometimes bears and mountain lions, kill calves.

But drought is the great uncertainty. "The worst drought in my lifetime started in '53," Joe Bill said. "There was no rain until '58. I was a kid but I remember how barren this land looked. A rancher doesn't fear anything more than he does drought. If it gets bad enough, you may have to sell all your cattle. It can take years to recover if you have to sell your breeding herd.

"There is so little you can do about drought. There's no control over what the good Lord will do. A farmer doesn't like rain during harvest, but we're grateful whenever it rains. Every year we gamble that it's going to rain, and we'll have enough forage for our livestock."

Whatever the gamble, the Nunn family has been ranching in New Mexico for more than fifty years. Smokey and Joe Bill each own their own land and lease some from the Bureau of Land Management —a total of about 130,000 acres—and they have their own brands. They keep separate books, buy land separately, sometimes buy and sell cattle separately. But many parts of the ranching operation they carry out together. They buy supplies together to get better volume prices. They sometimes sell cattle together because buyers want to buy larger quantities. Branding and most of the other ranch work are joint operations.

Joe Bill, his wife, Lauren, and their teenage son and daughter,

The Nunns: Joe Bill, Lauren, Justin, and Tami Jo.

Justin and Tami Jo, live in a large house on the ranch. Joe Bill, Lauren, Smokey, and one Mexican helper built the house in 1972, a task that took almost a year since they had time to work only at night and on the few rainy days when ranch work was halted.

"I did everything," Lauren told us, "drove nails, poured concrete, helped put shingles on the roof."

"Everyone works on a ranch," Joe Bill said. "There is always something to do."

Three hired hands are on the payroll, but the ranch is truly a family business. Lauren, Justin, Tami Jo, and Smokey's wife, Eunice Dean, are all good riders and help out whenever they are

A break in the action.

*Bucky McCauley, one of the cowboys on
the Nunn ranch.*

needed. The work rolls around from season to season, never ending: branding, moving cattle to different pastures for better grazing, mending fence, windmill repair, supplementary feeding, vaccinating and doctoring sick animals, hunting predators, culling and shipping.

"The whole year you've got to be watching them," Joe Bill said, talking about cattle. "You can't just put them out to pasture and go get them when you need money. You have to move them. You have to keep them away from poison weeds. You have to show them where water is; otherwise they'll get hung up in a fence corner and die of thirst. Sometimes calves will crawl under a fence and get separated from their milk and starve. During calving season we have to be extra watchful. Every few days we get a horse and ride pastures just to look the cattle over. You take care of them so they'll take care of you."

Justin and Tami Jo have their own brands. In the world of ranching that is very important. They are old brands that have been in the family for a long time and are registered with the New Mexico Livestock Board. Justin inherited his brand, the 2 Slash (2/) from his maternal grandfather; it was left to him in his grandfather's will. Tami Jo's brand, Bar 9 (−9) was given to her by Smokey as a Christmas present.

Tami Jo is seventeen, a junior in high school. She loves basketball and wants to be a basketball coach someday. She plans to study education in college and would like to go either to Texas Tech or New Mexico State University. But Tami Jo is sure that at some time in the future she will be a rancher.

Justin is not so sure. He likes town, wishes he lived in Deming, the county seat twenty miles from the ranch, where he is a senior in high school. Many nights, when the ranch work is done, he drives his pickup into town to be with his friends. He thinks right now that he doesn't want to be a rancher, that he would like to get out on his own and see the world. And yet in the back of his mind he is already thinking that he might borrow some money and buy a small ranch somewhere away from the family, somewhere on his own.

Justin says, "While I'm out riding sometimes I say to myself, 'This is something I can do well. This is cool.'"

The Fence

ZAY CLOPTON is a solidly built, muscular man with a bushy mustache adorning a face permanently reddened by the bright New Mexico sun. Zay, his wife, Nancy, and their seven-year-old daughter, Kristin, live on a Luna County ranch that stretches along the U.S.-Mexican border for almost ten miles. They are isolated. The nearest neighbor is six miles away; they do their shopping in Deming, sixty miles from the ranch; Nancy drives Kristin forty miles to school every day—160 miles of driving a day if she makes two round trips. But they live happily in a beautiful house they built themselves; and, except for one thing, Zay loves being a rancher here on the northern edge of the high Chihuahuan Desert.

The one thing Zay does not like is having to maintain the international boundary fence between the United States and Mexico that the U.S. government put up almost eighty years ago. We visited Zay at his ranch one morning to talk about the fence.

"The government doesn't care if the fence exists or not," he said. "At least, that's what they say. But the way it works out, they make me maintain the fence because if my cattle drift into Mexico, I can't just go and bring them back. They'd have to be quarantined first. And I've lost cattle over there that I've never seen again. Mexican ranchers don't worry about a fence. They don't care if their cattle come north, because they know their cows will be returned and will be on better feed for awhile over here. Mexican quarantine laws are lax, and Mexican health standards are nonexistent. That's the reason our laws are so strict for imported cattle. If Mexican cattle with some disease like brucellosis came through a hole in the fence and infected dairy cattle on this side of the border, it could cost millions of dollars and ruin a lot of New Mexico cattlemen."

History bears out what Zay Clopton says. In 1907 a presidential proclamation called for an international boundary fence between the

United States and Mexico to help prevent the spread of cattle disease. Between 1908 and 1910 the government built 698 miles of barbed-wire fence on the border between New Mexico, Arizona, and California and the Republic of Mexico. Later strong chain link fence was put up in the urban areas and carefully maintained by the Border Patrol; but as years passed, government maintenance of the barbed-wire fence in much of the rural desert area of the border declined.

At one time the U.S. Department of Agriculture repaired the fence in some areas, but it no longer does so, citing lack of funds as the reason. The government's International Boundary and Water Commission once helped maintain the fence but says that it "lost jurisdiction" thirty years ago. The Customs Service gives no help in border fence repair because the barbed wire does not deter smugglers, who simply cut it or climb over it. Similarly, the Immigration and Naturalization Service does not consider the barbed-wire fence a "people fence." The Mexican government has never been interested in spending money to maintain a fence between the two countries.

The result of this governmental neglect is that long stretches of the eighty-year-old border fence are in terrible condition. Fence posts have rotted; wire has rusted and sagged; in places the fence is lying on the ground or has disappeared entirely. It has been left to border ranchers like Zay Clopton to maintain a good fence between the United States and Mexico.

We got in Zay's pickup and drove down to the border to see the fence. The road was the worst we had ever been on. Zay said it was an old mining road that is used now by drug runners coming north from Mexico. We passed the ruins of the International Mine; in its heyday it produced lead, zinc, and silver. Mesquite thorns raked our truck as we drove by. We stopped at several watering places, and Zay dropped off heavy blocks of supplemental nutrients for cattle that stood around in the brush watching him.

"Have to give them supplement," Zay said, as we drove on, "but this country isn't as barren as it looks." And then he made a point similar to the one Joe Bill Nunn had made. "That's the miracle of cattle. They take land totally useless to man and they manufacture beef. They find a lot to eat out there."

Zay Clopton and the old border fence.

We finally reached the fence. This was a section of old fence that Zay has not yet had time, or money, to replace, but he has put in some new posts to keep it from falling down. "This fence was not built by the government," Zay said. "It was put up by a rancher in 1918."

We came to a new section of fence, six-and-a-half miles of it that Zay built in 1984. "Ray Sadler—he's head of the New Mexico Border Commission—got the state to put up $10,000 for materials. I supplied the labor."

Zay estimates that the fence would have cost $5,000 a mile, over $35,000, if he had not done the work of putting it up. "Took us four days to do a mile," he said, "in the hottest part of the summer. That was a month of work I could have been doing other things."

The new border fence. "This will last a long time."

But the new fence is a thing of beauty—six-and-a-half miles of steel post supporting six strands of tautly stretched new barbed wire. Every quarter mile larger posts set in concrete give additional support.

Zay stood looking at his new fence. "This will last a long time," he said with satisfaction.

We drove down the fence, and Zay showed us where it has already been cut six times by drug smugglers, holes big enough to drive a truck through. "It's a nuisance for me, having to work the fence over so often," Zay said. "The Border Patrol or Customs Service sure don't catch many of them."

A bit farther on we came to a place where a kind of informal gate had been made in the fence. "My Mexican neighbor made that," Zay said.

His rancher neighbor in Mexico, we learned, uses this gate freely, driving to the U.S. border town of Columbus to do his shopping, then returning through the gate to avoid the time and trouble of going through customs in the Mexican border town of Palomas. Much of this informal crossing goes on along the border.

"A man has to be a good neighbor," Zay said, looking at the gate in his new fence.

Smuggling: The Crime of Borders

NOT ALL PORTS of entry on the U.S.-Mexican border are big, bustling metropolitan areas like Tijuana-San Ysidro, Mexicali-Calexico, and the two Nogales. In Luna County, New Mexico, the U.S. entry port is the village of Columbus; it has a population of seventeen hundred. Its Mexican sister village in Chihuahua is Palomas, with about three thousand residents. Towns don't count their people in big numbers

Jorge Lona and confiscated vehicles used by smugglers.

in this high plains country where fifty to seventy acres will barely provide enough grass for one cow. But size doesn't always tell the story: more cattle cross into the United States through Palomas and Columbus than through any other port of entry on the border.

Jorge Lona is Director of Customs for the Mexican government in Palomas. A small man of ample girth, Lona is full of energy and moves with an easy grace I would not have expected. He looked at the white tennis hat I was wearing as protection against the border sun. "You play tennis, Mr. Brent?" he asked.

"I do," I told him, "enthusiastically but not well."

"You ever hear of Pancho Segura?" Lona asked.

Segura was one of the great professional tennis players of thirty years ago. "I saw him win a tournament once," I said.

"I used to play him," Lona said. "Almost every day. Next time bring your racket, and we will play a set."

I tried to imagine myself playing tennis against Pancho Segura. "If you spot me five games and forty love," I said.

Lona laughed and said, "What shall we talk about?"

We asked about cattle. "Oh, yes," Lona said. "This is the place where the most cattle cross. Chihuahuan cattle are very fine. Ranchers drive them here from all over Chihuahua, like cattle drives in the old West. They go into pens, not far from here. We keep count because there is a quota. Fifteen hundred to two thousand every day, 125,000 perhaps in a season. U.S. health inspectors check them before they cross, even blood tests. They must be in perfect health."

"Are cattle ever smuggled across the border?" I asked.

Lona gave us a rapid-fire minilecture on smuggling. Everything is smuggled on the border, he said, everything that people on either side place value on. Smuggling by definition is sneaking something across a border, from one country to another, without paying export or import duty, or sneaking something in that wouldn't be allowed under any conditions—drugs or guns, for example. Smuggling is a crime that happens only on borders.

All of my previous thinking and talking about smuggling had been about drug smuggling into the United States. "Is there much smuggling from the United States into Mexico?" I naively asked Lona.

He looked at me with astonishment and then jumped from his chair. "Come," he said. "I will show you."

He took us to a large cinder-block warehouse stacked with a jumble of typewriters, television sets, radios, tires, calculators, and a wide assortment of other products. "All these things were taken from people trying to bring them into Mexico without paying customs duty," he said. "I have thirty to forty agents working our side of the border. Smugglers try to come through at different places and sometimes right here through Palomas."

Lona asked one of his assistants to show us a large butane tank. "It came through here on a truck," the customs director said. "You

Smugglers concealed guns and bullets in this butane tank.

learn when to be suspicious. We looked carefully. It was full of guns and ammunition, not gas."

Lona took us out into a large parking area holding all kinds of vehicles: cars, trucks, vans, even a school bus. "We have confiscated all of these," he said, "taken them away from smugglers."

He showed us a van with the top ripped open. "Full of guns," he said. "Overhead and in the seats is where most contraband is hidden."

"The school bus," I said, "was it actually used for smuggling?"

"Oh, yes," Lona said. "Many seats for hiding things."

"I hope there weren't any children in it," I said.

"No children," he said. "I am glad."

98

A house in Palomas.

A Palomas family.

AFTER WE LEFT the customs office, we looked around Palomas. The look didn't take long: the single main street had a pharmacy, a steak house, the Lucky 7 Bar, Tillie's Curio Shop, and a few other places. The side streets were unpaved and dusty, the houses dilapidated and without plumbing. I remembered reading a tourist guidebook that called Palomas a picturesque little Mexican border town.

We walked back across the border to Columbus. It is an ordinary-looking little Western town, but it does have a unique place in American history as the site of the last hostile action by foreign troops inside the continental United States. On the morning of March 9, 1916, Columbus and nearby Camp Furlong, a U.S. Cavalry base, were attacked by the Mexican bandit and revolutionary, Pancho Villa, and about a thousand men under his command. After half a day of fighting, Villa and his forces fled back to Mexico but only after seventeen American civilians and soldiers and 142 of Villa's men were killed.

Villa's motive in making the raid seems to have been to embarrass President Woodrow Wilson for recognizing a Mexican president Villa opposed. In the wake of American national outrage over the unprovoked attack, President Wilson ordered General John Pershing to pursue Villa in Mexico. Pershing and his troops chased Villa for almost a year, fighting several skirmishes but never having a showdown battle. In early 1917, with America's entrance into World War I imminent, President Wilson called off the pursuit of Villa. Pershing went on to lead the American Expeditionary Force in Europe in the First World War.

In 1959 the Pancho Villa State Park was created on the site of old Camp Furlong, and suggestions have been made that the statue of Pancho Villa in Tucson should be transferred to Columbus. But many local citizens, including a few whose parents were there during Villa's raid, have different feelings.

Allen P. Borde is a rancher near Columbus who serves as municipal judge in the village. "Don't give us your statue," he said emphatically. "We don't even want that bandit's name on our state park."

III

THE RIVER
BORDER

TEXAS

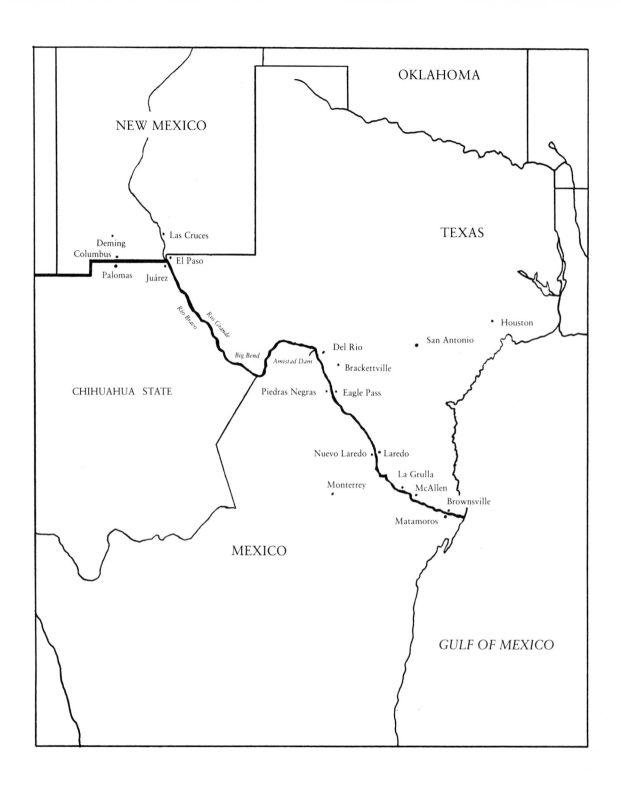

FROM ITS SOURCE in the San Juan Mountains of southwestern Colorado until it pours into the Gulf of Mexico, the Rio Grande is 1,885 miles long. It flows south through New Mexico, enters Texas at the state's most western extreme, and forms 1,254 miles of international boundary between the United States and Mexico. It is one of the longest river borders between two countries. But the name Rio Grande does not appear on maps made in Mexico. South of the border the great river is called the Rio Bravo.

A river border is different from an imaginary line or fence between countries. A river brings people together. They come to the river from both sides because of its water. They build towns along its banks and divert its water to irrigate farms and orchards. More than most rivers, the Rio Grande has attracted people because it is a green ribbon of life cutting through a desert. Long before the Rio Grande was a border, people lived along its banks.

If a river brings people to it, bridges across the river unite them. There are many bridges across the Rio Grande. Some are huge like the Good Neighbor Bridge in El Paso with its nine vehicle lanes and immigration and customs control. Many are tiny footbridges built by villagers where the river cuts its way through remote and lonely country. Such bridges are so insignificant that customs and immigration officials pay no attention to them, even if they know they are there. But these bridges, perhaps more than the great ones, bring people and families together in places where the border has little meaning in the way life is lived every day.

The Pass
to the North

WITH MORE than half a million people, El Paso is the largest U.S. city directly on the border. Ciudad Juárez, El Paso's sister city across the Rio Grande, is growing so fast that no one really knows its population. Ten years ago it was about the same size as El Paso; now demographers estimate that more than a million people live there. Together, the two cities are by far the largest metropolitan complex sharing the U.S.-Mexican border.

El Paso is located in an ancient mountain pass, and its early name, *El Paso del Norte*, describes exactly what it was and still is: the pass to the north. Since it was founded in 1827, untold millions of Mexicans have poured through El Paso, many millions of them to remain permanently in the United States. El Paso is the busiest port of entry on the U.S.-Mexican border. Each day the port clears over 650 commercial vehicles through U.S. Customs, and each year clears more than 35 million people through U.S. Immigration.

"But El Paso is not just a funnel that people and products pass through," Pablo Salcido told us. "It is the hub of an integrated economic unit that includes Juárez and Chihuahua in Mexico and Las Cruces and Alamogordo in New Mexico."

We were sitting in Pablo's office in the handsome new Civic Center Plaza in downtown El Paso. Pablo is Director of the Office of Economic Development for the City of El Paso, a big job for a young man just turned twenty-eight. Pablo was born and raised in El Paso, one of eleven children, but his mother and father were born in Mexico.

"My father worked for thirty years for the same company here in El Paso," Pablo told us. "He knew all the operations, but when time came for a promotion, he wouldn't get it. He would be passed

106

Every morning "burros" carry illegal workers across the river from Juárez to El Paso. The price is one dollar a trip.

Pablo Salcido and his fiancée, Cheryl Geurin, at the home of his parents.

over in favor of an Anglo. That isn't so likely to happen now. We are protected by civil rights laws. Our city leadership has matured. They say to themselves, 'If we don't give Mexicans skills and opportunities —open doors—our city won't grow.' Sure, it's self-interest, but it brought change."

Pablo talked further about his family. "Mom speaks very little English. We—my brothers and sisters and I—were completely Americanized; we wanted our parents to move to a nicer neighborhood. One of my brothers even bought them a new house. They refused to move. For a while, we—the children—were unhappy, maybe angry, but finally my dad made us understand that this was their life. Who

108

was Mom going to talk to in a new house in a new neighborhood? We apologized for thinking about ourselves, not them. They are happy, living where they have always lived."

Speaking once more of his father, Pablo said with obvious pride, "He showed us the importance of work, and he taught us to respect other people and the law."

Pablo exemplifies the generation of talented young Hispanic leaders that is emerging in the border cities. He understands and appreciates his Mexican heritage—the strong family tradition, the importance of religion, the belief in the reward of honest labor—and at the same time he understands and appreciates the fact that he is an American. After finishing his undergraduate study at Austin College in Sherman, Texas, Pablo decided to join the Peace Corps.

"I knew I wasn't ready for graduate study," Pablo said. "I wasn't very sure of myself, but I wanted to try to make it in the Peace Corps."

Pablo was sent to Honduras as a Peace Corps volunteer in 1978. He calls his two-and-a-half years there "an incredible maturing experience." He was assigned to a land reform program, and his work with peasant farmers opened his eyes to the problems of poverty and politics in Central America. After the Peace Corps, Pablo entered the Lyndon B. Johnson School of Public Affairs at the University of Texas and earned a master's degree. Then followed two years with the San Antonio Department of Economic Development, which was excellent preparation for his El Paso position. Pablo was recently named by *Texas Business Magazine* as one of Ten Rising Stars in Texas.

One of our visits to Juárez was with Pablo. "The Juárez city government has an annual budget of $20 million to work with," Pablo said as we drove through the crowded streets. "With half as many people, El Paso has $157 million.

"We have a revolutionary impact on northern Mexico," Pablo continued. By "we" he meant the United States and particularly U.S. border cities. "Mexicans in the border states see our development— our schools, our hospitals, our roads, our big new buildings—and they say, 'Why can't we have that, too?' Imagine what it must be like

Slums like these ring the Mexican border city of Juárez.

sitting in a shack on this side of the river and watching a new bank going up a mile away across the river? They look across the river every day and see all that opulence and think about what life is like over there.

"The people of Chihuahua—I mean the state—are very progressive and hardworking, very creative. They live in the same arid land that we do in Texas. So to survive they have to work hard. The geographical proximity to the United States is a great incentive to Chihuahuans and a great blessing, too."

Another time we went to a Juárez slum, Colonia Morrelos, with Abelardo Muniz, a Mexican graduate student at the University of Texas at El Paso. Many of the people who live in such slums are called *parachutistas* (parachutists) because they come in suddenly, stay a short time, and then are gone, either across the border or to

110

some other slum where they think their luck will be better. They are part of the great migration from the south, brought by hopes of jobs in the *maquiladoras* or dreams of better jobs in the United States.

But not everyone comes and goes quickly. We talked with a man and woman who, with their son, had lived for six years in a decrepit little house in Colonia Morrelos. They had come north from Torreón, a city in the state of Coahuila, because, they said, the border offered hope for them. But the hope came to nothing. Like many other families in their area, they have spent their years in Juárez as garbage pickers. Every night they go to the city dump and pick through the daily leavings. Their harvest is aluminum cans, cardboard, and occasionally some piece of clothing that can be sold for a few pesos. The son crosses the border every day to pick in the much richer garbage dumps of El Paso, but the father does not cross the border. He is too old and tired, and he does not see a promised land beyond the river that he once saw.

The problems of Juárez and most other Mexican border cities are severe, but they are not problems that stop at the border. "Both sides of the river are tied together in so many ways," Pablo Salcido said, echoing the words of Mayor Marcelino Varona in Nogales. "We have cousins, uncles, aunts who live in Chihuahua. I can't pretend they don't exist. We can't talk about Mexican and U.S. problems as though they are separate—not here, we can't. It's *our* health, *our* economy, *our* school system, *our* unemployment, *our* acquifer. We drink the same water!"

Happy Endings

EVERY BORDER city has its share of sad and happy stories about illegal aliens. Sad stories outnumber any other kind, but in El Paso we saw some happy endings unfolding. Oscar Miguel Etienne-Huembas, his wife, Mercedes, and their four children, ages eleven, ten, four, and two, escaped from Nicaragua in July, 1985. He was an official in a political party opposed to the ruling Sandanista government, and life had become intolerable for him and his family. There were constant threats against them, and Oscar knew the time would come when he would be put in jail or killed.

He had saved a little money, so they were able to slip out of Nicaragua and travel by bus through Mexico to the border city of Matamoros. There they illegally entered the United States at Brownsville, Texas, but not before a Mexican immigration official made them pay $60 a person. After getting the money, the official, to show what a kind man he was, led them to a place where they could wade across the Rio Grande.

Oscar and his family went first to Houston and then to Reno, Nevada, where he has a sister. He wanted to be a legal resident of the United States and hired a lawyer to help him apply to the Immigration and Naturalization Service for asylum as a refugee. But the lawyer proved to be of no help, and the INS told him to go back to Nicaragua. Oscar knew it was only a matter of time before he would be arrested, so he and his family set out again by bus, this time hoping to reach Miami, Florida. Thousands of Nicaraguans have sought refuge in Miami; Oscar knew many of his countrymen were there and hoped to find help.

But when the bus stopped in El Paso, the family's luck ran out. They were arrested by the Border Patrol and held in the El Paso detention center. Oscar applied for asylum as a refugee, which meant that he and his wife would be entitled to a hearing in an immigration court. But the court was jammed with cases, and four months went by while Oscar and Mercedes waited their turn. The detention center had no facilities for families. Mercedes and the children were held in one building, Oscar in another, and during their months in detention, they saw each other only a few times.

We were in immigration court the day the Etienne-Huembas' deportation hearing came up. They probably did not know how remote their chances of success were. Of all the thousands of requests for asylum by refugees from Guatemala, Nicaragua, and El Salvador,

Oscar and Mercedes Etienne-Huembas taking an oath to tell the truth at their deportation hearing.

less than one percent have been approved. The odds against Oscar and his family were more than a hundred to one.

Those odds seemed even greater after a short opening statement by presiding Immigration Judge Robert L. Erwin. He referred to the large number of people who are in the United States illegally and the necessity of dispensing justice efficiently, and he concluded, "One sad aspect of my job is that I frequently have to send back people who are nice."

He seemed to be talking about Oscar and Mercedes and their four children; but the hearing progressed, and the judge listened to testimony from Oscar and examined evidence of danger the family

Oscar and his son after they are reunited.

faced if they were returned to Nicaragua. In the end, Judge Erwin ruled that the Etienne-Huembases could remain in the United States as refugees. Their long ordeal of flight and hiding was over.

That night we saw them again at their temporary lodging in the home of a church worker. This was their first time together as a family since they had been put in the detention center. While the children sat around a television set and Mercedes helped clear dishes from the supper table, we talked to Oscar.

"I felt reborn in court today," he said, "knowing I would be reunited with my family and knowing that I had become a free man."

Oscar's plan was to continue on to Miami where he was sure he could make a decent living for his family. He hopes someday to be able to return to Nicaragua, but he does not know when that will be, if ever.

114

Nora Ramos and daughter in their El Paso home.

ANOTHER NIGHT we visited the home of Ignacio and Nora Ramos and their two daughters, Karla, eight, and Alejandra, seven. Ignacio and Nora were married in El Paso in 1976. At that time Ignacio's father was living in El Paso as a legal alien, and Ignacio and Nora visited El Paso on a temporary crossing permit for the wedding. They had fully intended to return to Juárez, but on a sudden impulse they decided to stay in El Paso.

"We were a little crazy, I guess," Ignacio told us.

He is an experienced tile setter and so was able to get regular work with building contractors. But the building trade is one that attracts many illegal aliens because the work is hard and there is need for unskilled labor. Border Patrol agents come frequently to construction sites to check the workers.

"They come around almost every day," Ignacio said. "One of

the hardest things I had to do was learn not to show I was afraid. I was nervous, so nervous, but I knew if I ran and tried to hide, I would get caught. That is what most illegals do, and the Border Patrol catches them. So when they came to where I was, I smiled and said hello and talked to them with my little bit of English. They always went on, but after they were gone, my knees would knock and I would be wet with sweat."

Ignacio and Nora began to make payments on a small house, but they always lived with the fear of being deported. "We told only our closest friends that we were here illegally," Nora said, "but we always had the feeling that the INS would catch us and make us go back to Mexico, and we would have to sell our house. I was afraid to go back to Juárez even to visit my family."

Finally, in 1983, they were caught, but they filed for a suspension of deportation. The request was denied, and their appeals for reconsideration were almost exhausted when a stroke of great good fortune entered their lives. Ignacio's father, who had lived in El Paso for fifteen years, became a naturalized U.S. citizen. Ignacio was now able to apply for legal residence under the family reunification portion of the immigration law. Usually there is a long wait for a visa, but Ignacio's application was approved promptly.

"It is wonderful to be free from fear," Nora said. "And it was wonderful to be able to go back to Juárez and see my family."

Karla and Alejandra are already U.S. citizens because they were born in El Paso. Ignacio and Nora are looking forward to becoming naturalized citizens at the end of the five-year waiting period. Both are going to night school to study English, which will help them in their daily lives and in their application for citizenship.

"And," Nora said, "our going to school sets an example for Karla and Alejandra. Education is so important."

AT TIMES we had the feeling that immigration law is an impersonal machine that grinds people up in its gears. But the cases of the Etienne-Huembases and the Ramoses showed us that the law can be administered with humanity; and we came across another case that

116

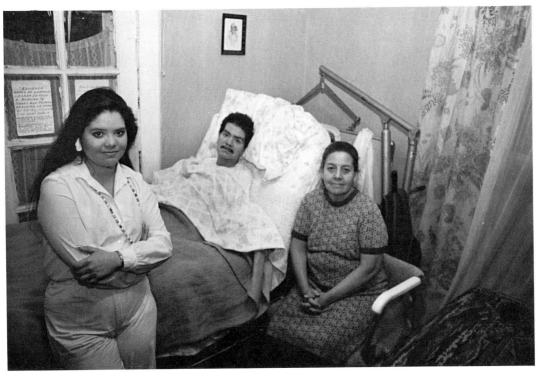

The Hernandez family.

made the point even stronger. The Hernandez family—the father, Ramon, the wife, Josefina, and their twenty-year-old daughter, Gloria Estela—were facing deportation as illegal aliens when Ramon became critically ill with multiple sclerosis.

In a strict interpretation of the law, Ramon's illness would have made no difference; the family would have been sent back across the border. But Ramon was granted a suspension of deportation on the grounds that he could receive better medical treatment in El Paso. Josefina's deportation was suspended so that she could provide the home care Ramon required. Gloria Estela was also given a suspension of deportation. The official reason in her case was to enable her to continue her education in the college where she is a student, but the humane reason behind the official one was clearly to keep the family together.

"I Get Aggravated and Nervous in Town"

THE BORDER COUNTRY between El Paso and Del Rio, 425 miles to the east, must be one of the loneliest parts of the United States. Yet in its immensity, it is surely one of the most awesome. A huge, arid land, tumbleweeds are thick, the wind blows incessantly, and dust devils twist across the empty landscape. Along the highway we passed Fasten Seat Belt signs with bullet holes in them, victims of casual target practice, and roadside picnic areas posted with Beware of Poison Snakes signs.

This is cattle country. For mile after lonely mile only an occasional windmill reminded us that people must live here. Around water holes we saw antelope mixing with cattle. After the urban throb of El Paso and Juárez, the scarcity of people was startling. The few towns along this stretch of the Rio Grande are tiny, none with more than two thousand people. The river is narrow here, the border guarded only by towering mountains on the Mexican side.

Halfway between El Paso and Laredo the Rio Grande changes its southeasterly direction, makes a great U-turn, and flows northeast for a considerable distance. This is the Big Bend, a place of towering mountains and spectacular canyons through which the fast-flowing river winds its way. Since 1944, eleven hundred square miles of mountains and desert within the *U* have been set aside as Big Bend National Park, a great wilderness area.

Despite its remoteness, thousands of visitors come every year to immerse themselves in the desolate beauty of this vast park. Cumulus clouds rest on top of the jagged Chisos Mountains. Shrubs and cacti cover the desert floor, interspersed with crowds of wild flowers during the spring and summer. Canoers paddle through the deep

118

The lonely border.

Pilots, who are stationed at Ft. Bliss, and their families enjoy a Sunday morning breakfast in Big Bend—100 yards from the Rio Grande.

canyons. The patient watcher can see desert mule deer, coyotes, foxes, peccaries, and, with great luck, perhaps a mountain lion.

For the bird watcher, Big Bend is the nearest thing to heaven. Over three hundred species inhabit its 750,000 acres at different times of the year. Paul is a passionate and totally dedicated bird watcher. One hot July morning, equipped with binoculars and two canteens of water, he set out for Boot Springs, high in the mountains. It is there, and only there in the entire country, that the shy, retiring Colima warbler sometimes can be seen. Just at nightfall when I was becoming concerned, Paul returned, weary, several pounds lighter, but a happy man. He had seen not one Colima warbler but two.

After the gigantic detour of Big Bend, the Rio Grande gets on about its business of reaching the Gulf of Mexico. The first sizable community on its banks after it is again on a southeasterly course is Del Rio. Jimmy and Katherine Sellers live in this bustling little city of thirty thousand, but their hearts and spirit are in the big country that surrounds it.

One day Jimmy took us to their sheep and goat ranch near the town of Comstock, northwest of Del Rio. The Sellers' River Ranch has eleven thousand acres and is home for twelve hundred goats and fourteen hundred Rambouillet sheep. The big, sturdy breed was developed in France, and the bucks have elaborately curved horns. The River Ranch was started by Jimmy's grandfather, who came from Tennessee in the early 1900s. Katherine's grandparents also came from Tennessee and settled twenty miles away. Their ranch, which Jimmy also manages, covers forty-five thousand acres. Jimmy's father still ranches on a piece of land east of Del Rio.

The Sellers have three children. The oldest son is following in Jimmy's footsteps and probably will be the fourth generation to manage the ranch. "We need help because I look after fifty-five thousand acres," Jimmy said. "I like doin' it, but it's hard to know from one year to the next what's going to happen. The droughts have made us cut back on our herds.

"No ranches around here are making any money now," he continued. "From '81 to '84 we had a drought and lost a bunch of money. This land doesn't have enough graze for cattle. I don't know

Jimmy Sellers feeds his goats.

how the straight cattle people stay in business. They haven't had a good year since the early seventies."

Everything in the rancher's world depends on rain, and it is a subject never far from Jimmy's thoughts. At the time of our visit rain had not fallen in seven months. "We were saved by an eight-inch snow in January," Jimmy said. "It gave the brush lots of life."

As our pickup bounced over the dirt roads that connect the watering tanks on his ranch, Jimmy pointed to a band of two-year-old sorrel horses running across the range. "They'll be broken sometime this fall," he said. "We'll keep some for rodeo horses and sell the others. I've tried to supplement our income with horses, but the price for them has turned down worse than it has for sheep and goats."

We had the feeling that Jimmy just enjoyed seeing the horses run across the range and would not have cared if he didn't make a dollar raising them.

We stopped to look at a tank which was almost dry. The watering tanks are shallow basins into which rain runs from the surrounding ridges and remains as a pond for stock to drink from. All the tanks on the ranch were dug by Jimmy's grandfather, and most of them are stocked with bass.

"They'll all be dry in a few months if we don't get rain," Jimmy said. He stared at the brown hills, monochromatic except for the feathery green of mesquite, and he added, "In this business you can hold off any economic problem if you have rain. If this country would stay wet for a week, it'd come back real quick. I don't know how it rebounds so fast, but it does."

We got back in the pickup and took off, brown dust trailing behind us like a jet's vapor. "There's lots of driving out here," Jimmy said. "We wear out a pickup every two years." He runs his pickup with a big tank of propane in the back.

Jimmy spotted a bunch of young goats and stopped to spread corn on the ground for them. "You've got to have a lot of food for a cow," he said as he worked, "but sheep and goats scrounge around and take care of themselves. They eat black brush, mesquite, cactus, grajia. But the kids need some looking after. They're very dependent.

124

You have to feed them grain, and you have to keep a lookout to see if they've got their hair caught in the cat-claw. That bush can just grab them and hold them 'til they die."

Jimmy finished his work and watched the kids eat the corn. "I like sheep and goats," he said. "Sometimes they get contrary, but we can always work 'em."

Jimmy told us that right now he sells Angora hair for $2.50 a pound—the market price is down—and it is milled in England and Japan. His goats average five pounds per animal. After the goats have provided hair for from five to seven years, the culling begins, and the culls are sold in Mexico.

"We market our lambs in July and August," Jimmy said. "They go to the East Coast. Just the old animals go to Mexico for tacos and tamales. They use the whole animal."

A crew of shearers comes up every year from Mexico to work the sheep. Most of them have legal papers for employment. "It's not worth it to work with illegals," Jimmy said. "Too much hassle."

He is apprehensive about Mexicans "taking over" on the U.S. side of the border. He doesn't have much faith in their ability to run things efficiently. He says there is a growing amount of prejudice among Anglos, especially young people, against Mexicans. The Anglos are good Christian folk who try to keep their prejudices in check, Jimmy insists, but they are uneasy about the future, especially when they see Hispanics winning so many local elections.

We returned to the pickup and drove for a while in silence. "I just love this land," Jimmy said after a few minutes. "I get aggravated and restless in town. It's not that I don't like people, but I like to get away from things out here. Two nights ago somebody stole our truck in town and drove it to Mexico. We were just plain lucky that the police caught the guy and we got it back. But it cost me lots of time and $120 to get the truck out of impoundment, and somebody still managed to steal the stereo."

Jimmy told us that one spring coyotes wiped out his father's kid crop. Another year a mountain lion broke the necks of twenty-nine sheep. "Just broke their necks," Jimmy said. "Didn't eat a thing. I figure it was a mama lion showing her young how to hunt. It hurt me, but we had to hunt them down and kill them. I didn't like to do it, but they cost me $20,000."

There is no doubt that Jimmy has deep feeling for the wild things that live on his land. Just before he turned the pickup around for the drive back, we saw the low silhouettes of a flock of wild turkeys running over a ridge.

"I don't let anybody hunt them," he said. "I want them to multiply."

He continued to look off into the distance, and once more his thoughts moved back to rain. "It's hard-looking country," he said, more to himself than to us. "But when it rains, it's real purty."

Water

IN A LAND where every drop of rain is precious, Del Rio has an almost unbelievable abundance of water. Just four miles to the south the Rio Grande forms the border with Mexico. San Felipe Creek winds its scenic way through the heart of the little city. On the outskirts of town, San Felipe Spring, for ten thousand years an oasis in the desert, flows 90 million gallons every day, providing Del Rio with cool, pure drinking water and irrigating surrounding farms.

Twelve miles to the west, Amistad Dam catches the water of the Rio Grande, and Pecos and Devil's rivers in a great reservoir. Amistad means "friendship," and the dam was built in a spirit of friendship as a joint project of the United States and Mexican governments. Lake Amistad covers 138 square miles and is shared by the people of both countries. Fishing is wonderful, and we were not surprised to find in the Del Rio telephone directory listings for the Amistad Bass Club, the Big Friendly Bass Club, and—at nearby Laughlin Air Force Base—the Military Bass Anglers Association.

Almost everyone we talked to in Del Rio had good feelings about living there. "It's a fine little town," Thomas Hubbell, com-

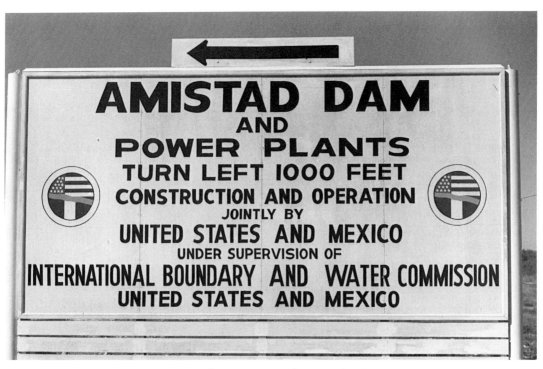

Amistad Dam near Del Rio and Falcon Dam, between Laredo and Matamoros, are two of the most important cooperative projects undertaken by the governments of Mexico and the United States.

munications director in the Del Rio Police Department, told us. A retired service man, Hubbell once was stationed at Laughlin Air Force Base and returned to Del Rio because he liked the town.

"The people are the best I've ever met," he said, "and I've been all over the world."

The same message of good feeling was delivered by Paul Kalinger, who owns a Del Rio furniture store. The walls of his cramped little office at the back of the store are filled with photographs of country music stars and other singers past and present: Elvis Presley, Johnny Cash, Dean Martin. The pictures are momentos of the days when Kalinger was a disc jockey.

"These are real friendly people," he said, talking about the residents of Del Rio. "You're not a stranger in this town. It's a slow-paced life, not much excitement. When they want to live it up, kids go up to San Antonio. And the water—the best drinking water in the world is right here."

We talked to Zina Worley who works in the Del Rio family planning office of the state Department of Health. She and her husband were stationed at Laughlin Air Force Base in the late fifties and came back to Del Rio when he retired.

"When we were living in Redlands, California," Zina said, "I read in the paper that our water coming out of the faucet was being recycled up to seven times, and I thought about Del Rio and the water from San Felipe Spring bubbling up out of the earth at the edge of town. But we came back to Del Rio because it is a real community that we could be a part of. That's important after years of living on Air Force bases. We like a bicultural environment. There's a lot of gentleness and kindness here.

"There has been genuine social integration since I arrived twenty-nine years ago as an Air Force wife. There was none in '57. At that time on the base there was a club for Hispanic women and one for Anglos. Now there is one club for all. In '58 I had a Mexican-American teacher and his wife to our house for dinner. Later he told me that he had never been in an Anglo house before. That kind of segregation or separation is a thing of the past now."

Zina talked about the river. "The most peaceful thing I've ever done in my life is float in the Rio Grande with a waterski belt wrapped around me. In the summer a friend and I go down to the river every day. We park one car downstream and the other upstream and float between them. We've floated for as long as four hours. It's as though you're alone in the world with birds, wind, and the sound of water. I wear a big straw hat. Everybody knows us along the way."

Zina spoke of the Western sense of distance. She thinks nothing of driving 150 miles to San Antonio to shop. "Maybe Del Rio is isolated," she said, "but I never think of it that way."

MOISES CALDERON'S hair is black; but to his legion of friends in Del Rio and all over the United States he is "Blondie," and he keeps two baby pictures of himself on the wall of Memo's Restaurant to prove that at one time in his life his hair was blond. Besides running the restaurant started fifty years ago by his father, Memo, and his mother, None (pronounced *no-ney*), Blondie is a professional musician. For twenty-seven years he has traveled with Ray Price as the famous singer's piano player.

"I never had any formal music training," Blondie said. "I've managed to hum a few bars, fake one here and there, and teach myself along the way. And I've been able to share what I learned with my own family and many others."

Every Tuesday night when he is in town, Blondie, his three daughters, and three brothers—all professional musicians—have a jam session at Memo's. The restaurant is standing room only on those nights, but it isn't just for the music. By general agreement, some of the best Mexican food to be found anywhere on the border comes out of Memo's kitchen.

Many famous musicians hungry for good Mexican food have come to Memo's; and when they come on Tuesdays, they usually take a turn in the jam session. Country and Western stars like Johnny Bush, Johnny Rodriguez, Jimmie Rodgers, Ray Price, and Willie Nelson have all dropped in for an *enchilada con huevo* or *chilie rellenos* and ended up jamming with Blondie. And not just famous musicians come. Blondie remembers his father's bullfighter friends coming from Ciudad Acuña, Del Rio's sister city across the Rio Grande, to eat at the restaurant. And Mama None can recall when "Mrs. Babe Ruth" came in for a meal.

But Blondie doesn't think just of famous names. In the past fifteen years scores of restaurants and fast-food places have sprung up along the twelve-mile stretch between Del Rio and Amistad Dam. "But you know," Blondie said to us. "People drive by all those places to come down here and eat."

Blondie is not unaware that Del Rio has many of the problems that beset all border towns. He talked about the large amounts of illegal money in the local economy that come from smuggling drugs and illegal aliens. He spoke of the extensive use of Mexican labor because the men and women from across the border would

Blondie Calderon with treats from Memo's kitchen.

work for less than the legal minimum wage. But still this little city is close to his heart.

"In twenty years of traveling with Ray, I've never found a place like Del Rio," he said. "It's where I want to live."

Memo's is located at the edge of San Felipe Creek. When Blondie isn't on the road with Ray Price, he likes to sit at his piano in the corner of the restaurant and play while he looks out at the lovely little stream.

The Tribe Without a Country

FIFTY MILES DOWN RIVER from Del Rio the little city of Eagle Pass has a good deal going for it. It is headquarters for Alta Verde Industries, a big cattle feedlot and packing plant operation. It is a major port of entry for Mexican products coming into the United States. Summer bullfights held in its sister city, Piedras Negras, attract visitors from all over the Southwest.

But Eagle Pass has a problem. Under the busy International Bridge that spans the Rio Grande and connects Eagle Pass with Piedras Negras lives a tribe of Kickapoo Indians. The former home of this southern branch of the Kickapoo tribe is El Nacimiento, a Mexican town in the Sierra Madre foothills, about 150 miles from Eagle Pass. But for the last fifty years most of the small tribe—about seven hundred men, women, and children—have lived in shacks and huts beneath the bridge for a part of every year.

The Kickapoo are migrant farmworkers, following the annual harvests of fruits and vegetables through Texas, into Colorado, and as far west as California, Oregon, and Washington. Some Kickapoo have made the village in Eagle Pass their permanent home, returning there after they finish their migrant work intead of going to Mexico. They journey to El Nacimiento only for religious events and to see relatives.

At Alta Verde Industries feedlots near Eagle Pass, cattle are fattened for six months before being shipped to buyers.

"They're squatters," one unhappy Eagle Pass merchant said to us. "They have absolutely no right to live under the bridge. But if the city government made them move, they'd just camp someplace else on the edge of town."

"Do they cause trouble?" I asked.

"They don't make trouble," the merchant said, "but their camp is a health hazard and an eyesore."

The village is indeed a sad sight. The shacks and huts are built of river reeds, scrap lumber, cardboard, pieces of tin, and anything else that can help hold out rain and wind. They have no electricity, no running water, no plumbing. Parked near the shacks are old pickup trucks and battered station wagons with tags from half a dozen agricultural states. On one side of the bridge under which the ragtag village sits is a public golf course, on the other side a busy downtown street.

The Kickapoo are another example of immigration rules and regulations being administered with flexibility. I asked a Border Patrol officer why his agency had never made an effort to keep the Mexican Kickapoo from crossing the Rio Grande to live and work in the United States.

"Who's to say who they are or where they belong?" he said. "Maybe they're Mexicans. Maybe they're Americans. They've been going back and forth across the border for over a hundred years. If they don't make trouble, we don't."

The Border Patrol officer knew some history. Long ago the Kickapoo, an Algonquin-speaking tribe, were pushed from New York by larger tribes. They trekked westward to Wisconsin but in the eighteenth century, under pressure from encroaching white settlers, moved to Illinois. From there, always trying to avoid the tide of white settlement, their wanderings took them into Missouri and Kansas. Finally, they were given a reservation in Oklahoma.

But part of the Kickapoo tribe resisted reservation life. They felt—and time proved them right—that the pressure from white settlers would continue. From the late 1830s until after the Civil War small groups of Kickapoo emigrated from Oklahoma to Mexico, making the long and sometimes hazardous journey across Texas.

Kickapoo huts in Eagle Pass.

In 1865, the last group to make the trip was attacked at Dove Creek by a company of citizen-soldiers who did not know the Kickapoo had received permission from the governor of Texas to cross the state. The Kickapoo suffered many casualties and never forgave the attack. For years afterward they raided Texas ranches and villages along the Mexican border.

The Mexican Kickapoo, as they came to be called, made their home near El Nacimiento. They hunted and fished and sometimes worked on Mexican ranches. They kept to themselves, seldom inter-marrying, and the Mexican government paid little attention to this small Indian tribe from across the border. Kickapoo children did not attend Mexican schools.

The Kickapoo did not complain. They were left alone to practice their tribal religion, to speak their own language, to instruct their children in the lore of the tribe. For these reasons they had come to Mexico.

Then, with the beginning of World War II, a new page was turned in the Kickapoo odyssey. The manpower shortage on U.S. farms caused by the war brought an urgent need for people to harvest crops. At first only a few Kickapoo came back across the border to harvest onions and pick cotton in south Texas, but in time most of the tribe joined the migrant farmworker streams in the United States and made their home under the bridge in Eagle Pass.

Poverty in Mexico pushed the Kickapoo back across the border, just as it has motivated millions of Mexicans to go to the United States. But the Kickapoo, even in the squalor under the International Bridge, have not forgotten who they are. One of the huts in the village is the sacred hut, where the children are taken every day at midday to learn the religion and ways of the tribe. A few years ago a terrible flash fire swept through the Kickapoo village, destroying almost everything. But the sacred hut was hardly touched and no child was injured. The Kickapoo rebuilt their village of river cane, scrap lumber, and cardboard shelters around the sacred hut.

PAUL AND I heard of the Kickapoo story when we visited Bud and Nakai Breen in their comfortable home in Brackettville, a small town near Eagle Pass. Bud met Nakai in Eagle Pass over thirty years ago when he was a cowboy working on the King Ranch. They married, raised a family of four boys and three girls, and Bud became a successful artist, drawing on his cowboy past for inspiration. His paintings are in the collections of such famous entertainers as Dean Martin, Roy Rogers, Jimmy Stewart, Richard Widmark, and the late John Wayne.

Nakai is an Indian, not a Kickapoo, but most of her life has been spent with the Kickapoo tribe. "I'm a Cherokee by birth," she told us, "a Kiowa by adoption, and a Kickapoo in spirit."

Nakai was born in the Cherokee town of Tahlequah, Oklahoma. She and her brother were raised by their grandmother; but when Nakai was twelve, they were adopted by a Kiowa Indian couple, who

Nakai.

Bud Breen at work.

took them to Eagle Pass. Nakai's memories of those early years are blurred in some ways but unusually vivid in others. She knows that her grandmother thought that she and her brother would have a better life with a foster mother and father who could provide well for them. Nakai's foster mother is still alive but won't talk about the adoption.

"I'm your mother," she has always told Nakai, shutting the door to the past.

Not long after Nakai came to live in Eagle Pass she saw a Kickapoo Indian for the first time. She and her brother were on their way to school one morning when she saw an old man and woman go to the door of a house near the school. Nakai stopped to watch them. They knocked on the door and, when it was opened by a woman, they asked for coffee.

"I can still hear their voices," Nakai said, "and I can still hear the woman in the house when she said, 'No Indios! No Indios!' as she slammed the door.

"I told my brother I was going to take the old man and woman home," Nakai continued. "I told him to go on to school. When they came down the steps from the house, I motioned for them to follow me and they did. Maybe something about the old woman reminded me of my grandmother. But it was more than that. There was something about her. I just wanted to help her.

"I took them home, but I was afraid of what my mother would say, so I knocked on the front door. When she came to the door, I was standing there with the old man and woman, and I said, 'Look what I've found.'

"My mother was shocked to see me with those two old Kickapoo when I should have been at school, and she said, 'You don't find *people*, Nakai.' And then I said, 'I want to adopt them.'

"My mother made me go back to school, and I wondered if I would ever see the old woman and the old man again. But when I got home from school that afternoon, they were still there. My mother had given them coffee and food, and they were just sitting there.

"I don't know what it was, but my heart just about burst. And when they left to go back to the Kickapoo village, I said to that old grandmother, 'I will go to school, and I will learn, and I will help you the rest of my life.' That's what I told her, those exact words. I don't know if she understood me then, but later I know she did. I never forgot her, and she was 102 when she died five years ago."

From that day when she met the old man and woman, Nakai became a Kickapoo in spirit. Almost every day after school and on weekends, she went to the Kickapoo village. She learned the Kickapoo language. She nursed sick people, cooked and washed clothes for them, found food and medicine for them in Eagle Pass. She took care of children so their mothers could work. She helped men and women search for jobs.

After she finished school, Nakai married Bud Breen and they raised a family in Eagle Pass, but Nakai did not forget the Kickapoo. She began to spend even more time working for the tribe, and the tribal council named her official representative of the Texas Kickapoo, as those living in Eagle Pass now called themselves.

The great problem of the Texas Kickapoo was that they were not recognized by the United States government as an American Indian tribe. They were not eligible for the educational opportunities, health care, and other benefits that are given to all tribes recognized by the Bureau of Indian Affairs. Although their northern cousins, the Oklahoma Kickapoo, had long been given official status, the Kickapoo who had gone to Mexico in the nineteenth century were not even American citizens.

Nakai spent years writing and calling congressmen, writing and calling officials in the Bureau of Indian Affairs, making radio and television talks, enlisting the help of private organizations in an effort to obtain government recognition for the tribe that she thought of as her own people. In large measure through Nakai's efforts, religious and educational groups in Texas and elsewhere became concerned with the problems of the Texas Kickapoo.

Finally, in 1983, Congress recognized the Mexican or Texas Kickapoo as a subtribe of the Oklahoma Kickapoo. They became eligible for citizenship, and immediately 150 chose to become U.S. citizens, making them eligible for federal benefits. In time probably most of the southern Kickapoo will choose U.S. citizenship, but for the

Bud and Nakai Breen with their adopted Kickapoo son, Kikakineta.

present many have held back. The rejection of the white man's world that a century and a half ago spurred the ancestors of these Kickapoo to choose life in Mexico instead of reservation life still flickers in the tribe. They are going to take their time.

Through the efforts of many private groups, money had been raised to purchase 125 acres of land south of Eagle Pass for the Kickapoo. The tract has been named Nuevo El Nacimiento, and all groups concerned with the health and well-being of the Kickapoo hope that it will become their permanent home.

"It's beautiful," said Bud Breen, speaking of the new land.

But so far no Kikapoo have moved there. Some of them say they want to move there, and in time perhaps most of them will make the move. But again some deep tribal instinct seems to be telling them not to rush in to being tied to this piece of land provided, with the best intentions, by white men. In the meantime, they continue to live under the International Bridge.

Nakai Breen has resigned as official representative of the Texas Kickapoo and has retired from active work with the tribe, but she still has many Kickapoo friends and helps many on an individual basis. "I am tired," she told us. "I have folded my hands."

But her hands are not quite folded. Recently she and Bud adopted a two-year-old Kickapoo boy, whose name is Kikakineta. She speaks to her adopted son in Kickapoo.

"I want to educate him so he will be a spokesman for the Kickapoo," Nakai said. "He is our sunshine now. Someday he will be the sunshine of his tribe."

Los Dos Laredos

IF THERE ARE more compatible cities on the U.S.-Mexican border than the two Nogales, they would have to be the two Laredos: Laredo, Texas, and Nuevo Laredo, its sister city across the Rio Grande. Before the Mexican War there was but one Laredo, and it was located on the north bank of the Rio Grande. When the town became a part of the United States after the war, residents who did not want to give up their Mexican citizenship moved across the river and named their new town Nuevo Laredo. They dug up the remains of their ancestors from the Laredo cemetery and took them to the new town for reburial. But they left relatives and friends in the old town, and a border has never been able to keep them apart.

Los dos Laredos: the two Laredos. City officials and businessmen seldom talk about one of the Laredos without talking about the

"Stretching" luxury cars into limousines in a Nuevo Laredo maquiladora.

other. In their efforts to bring in *maquiladoras* and other businesses and industries, they emphasize the cultural closeness of the sister cities, the big consumer market because people from both sides of the river mingle so freely, and the big, stable labor force which both cities contribute to.

Laredo and Nuevo Laredo are also tied together by an international transportation network that no other border city can equal. A major U.S. highway, Interstate 35, begins almost at the Canadian border and ends in Laredo. The Pan American Highway begins in

142

Nuevo Laredo and continues through Mexico, Central America, and South America. The Union Pacific Railroad connects Chicago and Laredo, and Nuevo Laredo is the main border terminus of the Mexican National Railway. With considerable justification, Laredo bills itself as the Gateway to Mexico. Every month over forty-five hundred loaded railway cars roll south into Mexico and ten thousand loaded trucks start their journey down the Pan American Highway from *los dos Laredos.*

Some people think there is no better evidence of the closeness of the two cities than the fact that they share a baseball team. *El Tecolotes* (the Owls) are technically the Nuevo Laredo franchised club in the Mexican Baseball League, a professional organization that includes teams from Mexico City, Guadalajara, Monterrey, and other Mexican cities. But the Owls play half their home games in Nuevo Laredo and half in Laredo. Immigration formalities are suspended when buses bring the Owls and the visiting team across the border for a game. No player is asked for a visa or a "green card" work permit before he takes his turn at bat.

Nuevo Laredo even takes part in the week-long Washington's Birthday Celebration that Laredo has held every year since 1898, by far the biggest celebration of its kind in the United States. In a ceremony on the International Bridge, U.S. and Mexican officials reaffirm the friendship of the two countries, then the citizens of Nuevo Laredo join enthusiastically in the parades, dances, feasts, games, and fireworks display.

We had a talk with Dr. Jerry Thompson, border historian and teacher at Laredo Junior College. He let his mind move around over a number of subjects. "The border," he said, "is not really Mexico and not really the United States either but part of each blended together. Take language, for example. A lot of what we hear on the border is not Spanish and its not English. We call it Tex-Mex. The other day I heard a native-Spanish speaker talking about 'el sidewalke.'"

All along the border we had seen and heard evidence of what Dr. Thompson was talking about. "Spanglish," the mixing of Spanish and English, it was called in some places. In Mexicali I remember a woman in a store talking about a dress and saying "*Esta muy*

Spanish and English melt together on the border.

nice." Talking with some Owls baseball fans we heard words like "bate" and "jon ron" for bat and home run. Such "corruptions" may horrify language purists, but most linguists are not alarmed. This is what happens when cultures mingle and people want to make themselves understood. And it is one way a language enriches itself with new words and expressions.

Dr. Thompson talked about the impact of the United States on northern Mexico. "I think much of the political unrest in northern Mexico is due to its proximity to us and our political processes," he said. "Upper-class Mexicans are greatly influenced by American TV,

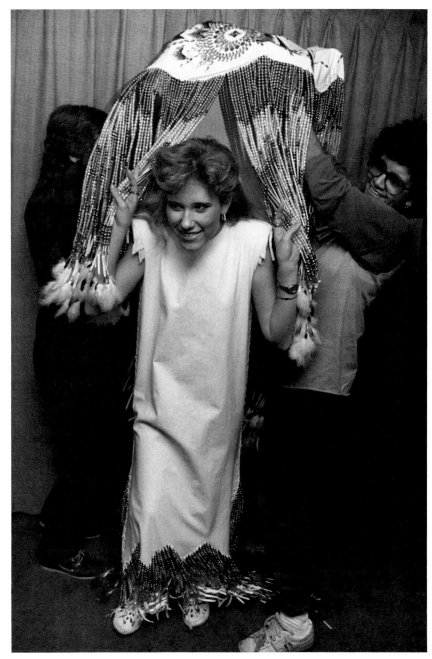

One of the Washington's Birthday Celebration events in Laredo is the honoring of Princess Pocahontas and her court. The 1987 Princess Pocahontas is Larissa Linnet Howell. Here she is fitting her pageant dress.

newspapers, and books. It is amazing to check into a Monterrey hotel and find that nine out of ten TV channels are U.S. stations. A middle-class person in Monterrey has much more in common with a suburbanite in San Antonio than he has with the *campesinos*, the farmers, outside his own city."

And shifting the focus a bit, Dr. Thompson continued. "The United States is to Mexico today what the American frontier was to the Eastern part of our country 150 years ago—a safety valve. If you shut that valve Mexico will burst as the seams. Laredo is the Ellis Island of the last part of the twentieth century."

WE UNDERSTOOD Dr. Thompson's comparison of Laredo to Ellis Island, but there is one huge difference. The men, women, and children who saw the Statue of Liberty when they landed at Ellis Island decades ago were all legal immigrants. Almost all of the immigrants pouring into Laredo from Mexico are illegal aliens who will be turned back if the Border Patrol catches them.

That afternoon we went to the Laredo railroad yard with Border Patrol Agent David Scherzer. Before joining the Border Patrol David was a welder who "got tired of looking at the world through a dark glass," but as a Border Patrol officer he sees plenty of the dark side of life. He drove us to Jefferson field, a trash-filled area near the upper end of of the freight yard.

"This place fills up at night with people who have come across the river and are waiting for a train to start," he said. "Crouched down in that grass or behind the trash, they can be ten feet from you and you can't see them, even with a flashlight. At the last minute, when the train starts up and there's an awful racket with the cars slamming together, they make a mad dash. We've seen fifty at once. The human wave, we call it. A rail yard is a dangerous place. Trains are big and move fast. It's easy to slip when you're trying to scramble onto a car. A month doesn't go by that we don't have an alien killed or cut up bad. But they know that if they can get on a train and ride out of here, they're in free. So they keep trying."

That night we came back to the freight yard, and soon the agents

146

Caught. A young Mexican illegal alien is flushed from his hiding place in the Laredo freight yard.

Alone and lonely in the Laredo detention center, this young Central American woman waits for her deportation hearing.

we were with found three Mexicans hiding in the brush. They routed a fourth out of a nearby freight car, a gondola. They were all between eighteen and twenty years old and had arrived in Nuevo Laredo that afternoon. Before swimming the river, the Mexican police had caught them and made them pay $8 apiece—all the money they had—to let them go.

Many illegals put their clothes in a plastic bag to keep them dry before they swim the river, but these young men hadn't done that. They were still wet and shaking with cold, or perhaps nervousness. I think they were glad to be caught, once they saw they weren't going to be hurt. They had no skills, but a friend in Austin had promised to find them jobs. One said he had wanted to go on to Chicago.

Catching illegal aliens is Border Patrol Agent David Scherzer's job, but he knows very well that they are human beings with very human feelings. "You have to imagine what it would be like to be hundreds of miles from home," David said, "and not have any real idea of where you are or what's out there in the dark waiting for you—what kind of unknown terrors. And your head is filled with all kinds of stories about what the Border Patrol is going to do to you if they catch you."

The Valley

WHEN A TEXAN talks about the Rio Grande Valley or just "the valley," he is talking about the southern tip of the state from about Rio Grande City in Starr County to the Gulf of Mexico twenty miles beyond Brownsville in Cameron County. Between those two counties is Hidalgo County. These three counties form the valley—some people add Willacy County to the north of Cameron County—approximately 110 miles of some of the richest agricultural land in the country.

Harvesting celery near La Grulla.

The valley is not really a valley but rather a fertile plain sloping away from the Rio Grande, like a delta. The slope is important because it simplifies irrigation of the forty-mile-wide band of alluvial soil that the river, over eons, has deposited on both banks. No one can tell you with any certainty why this little tip of South Texas is called the valley, but it has been since anyone can remember.

When you enter the valley from the west, you leave behind the dry arroyos, the tumbleweeds, the brown hills. You are suddenly in a subtropical land of citrus orchards, palm trees, and a humid climate that allows a 330-day growing season every year. "The Winter Garden of the Nation" the valley is often called, and its winter vegetables and citrus are shipped all over the country. Cotton, sugarcane, corn, grain sorghum, melons, and livestock are also important valley products.

Although it might seem to be a kind of Garden of Eden, the valley is one of the poorest areas in the United States. Its unemployment level of 15 percent is twice the national rate, and a per capita income of just over $4,000 is half the national average. Starr County ranks at the very bottom as the poorest county in the entire nation.

We knew that sudden freezes in winter can wipe out a valley crop overnight and that hurricanes off the Gulf can leave a flattened mess in the fields. We also knew that prices of farm products have not been good in years and that costs of fertilizer and machinery are high. But those things could not explain the amount of poverty in the valley, and to try to get a better understanding we talked to Dr. Antonio Zavaleta in Brownsville. Dr. Zavaleta is Director of the South Texas Institute of Latin- and Mexican-American Research at Texas Southmost College.

"Agriculture here is agribusiness," he said. "Families don't own land anymore. Most of the valley now is owned by European and Japanese corporations. Because of mechanization there are fewer jobs. *Maquiladora* money spills over the border for merchants, but jobs are mostly on the Mexican side. The economy of the valley has always depended on great numbers of cheap Mexican workers. Illegal immigration hurts us but at the same time keeps our economy afloat because employers can hire cheap labor.

152

This maquiladora *in Matamoros is owned by Fisher-Price Toys.*

"The population of the valley is the fastest growing in the country. The fertility of Hispanics is the highest in the United States, and four out of every five persons in the valley is Hispanic, mostly Mexican ancestry, of course. That means more young people to support and more young people coming into the job market."

Dr. Zavaleta seemed to be describing the prevailing Third World condition of too many people and not enough jobs.

"Well over 50 percent of the valley's population falls below the poverty level," he continued. "This has been true ever since Brownsville was founded in the middle of the nineteenth century. There is a tradition of poverty here, and today there are more poor people who are poorer than they ever have been.

"The greatest industry in the valley is the poverty business: food stamp programs, health clinics, welfare workers, other government subsidized programs. Poverty is an institution. The valley can't live without it."

He handed us some figures to prove his point. They showed that city, state, and federal government jobs in the valley outnumbered agricultural jobs by four to three.

Before we left, Dr. Zavaleta talked about border relationships, especially in terms of Matamoros, Brownsville's sister city. "Businesses on both sides are intermeshed through partnerships," he said. "Families are interwoven, intertwined. I have many, many relatives in Matamoros. To us the river has never been a boundary. We are not separated by it. It unifies us."

Dr. Zavaleta's explanation of poverty in the valley was easier for us to understand because of a stop we had made in the little town of La Grulla in Starr County before we reached Brownsville. We had been in La Grulla two years before when we were gathering material for our book about migrant farmworkers and at that time had met Diana and Joel Villarreal and their daughter, Marlen. Although they did not know we were coming now, we hoped to see them again.

They were still there and still living in their snug little house near the highway, but an important change had taken place since our last visit. At that time, Diana was pregnant. Since then Joel, Jr., had arrived and was making his presence very much known around the house.

Diana and Joel are fond of their house, which Joel built with the help of his father, but they have rarely been able to live in it for a whole year at a time. Like most of the families in La Grulla, the Villarreals are migrant farmworkers, and almost every year in April they close their house, pack their station wagon with clothes, blankets, dishes, and food, and make the long drive to Washington State, where for several months they labor in the fields cutting asparagus and picking strawberries.

The Villarreal family.

As children, Joel and Diana had worked in the fields with their migrant parents, following the harvests from state to state, returning to La Grulla in the fall. Both Joel and Diana had graduated from high school, which few migrant children are able to do. After they were married, they had hoped to build a life that would not mean moving themselves and their children around the country from one harvest to the next.

For three years after their marriage Joel was able to find enough work in the nearby city of McAllen to enable them to live in La Grulla year round and stay out of the migrant stream. But with the devaluation of the Mexican peso, jobs became scarcer and pay poorer. The time came when there was no money to buy food or

155

clothes or to pay their small house bills; the only answer was to go back on the road as migrant farmworkers.

They were about to begin their fourth year of migrant work when we met them the first time. Now we learned that tragedy had struck the morning after we left La Grulla.

"We were packed and ready to leave that morning," Diana said. "My father was going with us. We were almost ready to get in the car when he shot and killed himself. I don't know why he did it. But he was so discouraged. He was so in debt."

Like so many farmworkers in the valley, Diana's father had spent much of his life in debt. She told us about one summer when her father and mother and their seven children had gone to work in the fields of Washington and Oregon. The summer was hard but profitable, and they had saved $18,000 from their labors. But her father had $16,000 in debts, so they had only $2,000 to show for months of backbreaking work.

"He was always having to borrow from one bank to pay another," Diana said. "My mother had to borrow $2,000 for the casket and the funeral."

Three days after the funeral Joel, Diana, and Marlen started the long drive to the asparagus fields. In Cortez, Colorado, their old car broke down, and much of what they earned the first month had to be spent to repair it.

Last year they had been able to stay out of the migrant stream because Joel had found construction jobs in McAllen and then in Corpus Christi and Houston. But now he was out of work again, and bills were piling up. Diana had had a miscarriage, and the hospital had charged her $1,500 for a twenty-four-hour stay. There seemed to be no choice but to close up their house and return once more to the road. This would be Joel, Jr.'s, first taste of migrant life.

"I don't want to go," Joel said, "but I must have work."

I am sure that no people on earth appreciate a home more than migrant farmworkers. One thing is certain. If Joel can find a way, the time will come when his family will live all year every year in their little house in La Grulla.

A street in Brownsville.

OUR BORDER journey ended in Brownsville. More than any other U.S. city we visited, Brownsville looks and feels like a city on the Mexican side of the border. We walked many of its streets without hearing a word of English. Most store signs are in Spanish. "Spanish Spoken Here" signs do not appear in shop windows. Of course Spanish is spoken if the merchant wants to stay in business. The owner of El Mundo, an electronic equipment store located a block from the Brownsville-Matamoros bridge, told us that 95 percent of his business comes from across the bridge.

Customs inspection, Port of Entry, Brownsville, Texas.

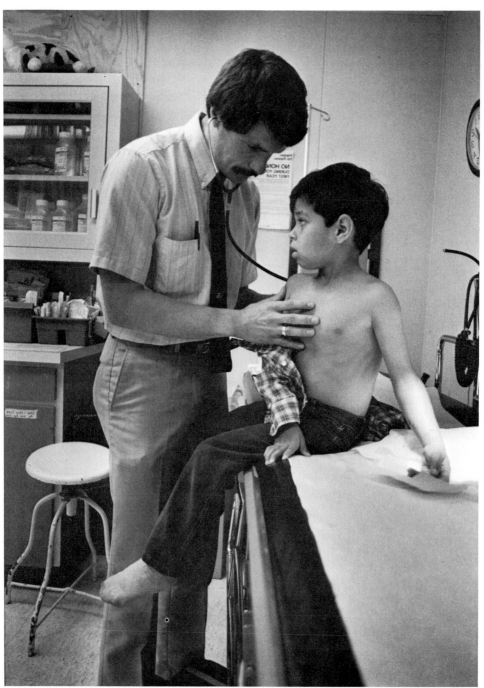

Dr. David Smith and patient at the Bronwsville Community Health Clinic.

Standing at the northern end of the bridge, we watched streams of women returning to Mexico heavily laden with shopping bags full of groceries. The parking lot of King Mart, a supermarket located near the bridge on the Brownsville side, was full of cars with Mexican license plates. One of the King Mart managers told us that the quality of the products is what brings the shoppers from Mexico—plus the fact that some items like toothpaste and even coffee are often hard to find in Matamoros. Mexican shoppers can pay in pesos in Brownsville stores.

We talked to Dr. David Smith, director of the Brownsville Health Clinic, about health care in Brownsville. His clinic is funded (or underfunded) by the federal government. Almost all the people who come to the clinic are below the poverty line and cannot afford to go to either of Brownsville's private hospitals. The clinic handles about 110,000 visits a year.

Cameron County, where Brownsville is located, accounts for an astonishing 10 percent of the nation's out-of-hospital births every year. People can't afford private hospital maternity care and go instead to *paternas*, as midwives are called in Spanish. Local hospitals require deposits of between $2,000 and $3,000 for maternity cases, and the poor can't find that kind of money. For a while Dr. Smith's clinic had a maternity section, but it had to close because there was no money to keep it open. Dr. Smith spoke of infants who died and were sent back to Mexico in boxes for burial. "Shoebox burials" he called them.

From one end of the border to the other, we heard of Mexican women crossing the border to have their babies in the United States. In that way the babies will automatically be U.S. citizens. But the shoebox babies will never take advantage of their American citizenship.

The last person we talked to in Brownsville was Alexandro Perez, an assistant superintendent in the city school system. "The equivalent of a new elementary school comes across the river every year," he said. He pulled a piece of paper out of his desk. "Look at this."

The paper showed that in the 1985-86 school year, the Brownsville system had been asked to educate 521 Mexican children who

Brownsville high school students.

were in the city illegally, 265 Mexican children there legally, and 736 children who were U.S. citizens because they had been born in the United States to Mexican mothers who then took them back to Mexico. Now they were coming across the border to be educated in Brownsville schools.

"Almost every day I hear parents say, 'We're here because we want to educate our children,'" Perez said. "Most of these parents can't speak English and that makes it hard for them to get jobs. They are determined that their children will learn."

Brownsville is too poor—not nearly enough tax money—to build the new schools needed and must resort to temporary portable classrooms. "They're temporary, but I'm afraid they're here to stay," an assistant principal at a neighborhood elementary school told us. This was a school where less than 1 percent of the students were

Anglo children. "Because of these temporaries, there isn't even enough money to air-condition our old main building."

Yᴇᴛ ᴀʟʟ ᴀʟᴏɴɢ the border, the people we had talked to—not all of them but most—did not feel anger or resentment at the way Mexico's problems of employment, health, and education spilled across the international boundary into the United States. In their own way most had echoed the words of Pablo Salcido in El Paso: "We can't talk about Mexican and U.S. problems as though they are separate— not here, we can't."

A New Immigration Act

Oɴ Oᴄᴛᴏʙᴇʀ 17, 1986, after five years of bitter debate, Congress passed a new immigration bill, which President Ronald Reagan promptly signed into law. The most important provisions of the new law are these:

—Employers who hire illegal aliens are subject to a fine of from $250 to $2,000 for each person hired. For repeated offenses an employer's fine could go as high as $10,000 per illegal alien hired, and the employer could be put in jail for up to six months.

—Employers must ask job applicants for documents which prove they are citizens of the United States or, if they are not, that they have a legal permit to work in this country. Birth certificates, passports, INS work permits, Social Security cards, and drivers' licenses are types of documents that might be used. The employer does not have to check the authenticity of the documents presented by a job applicant.

—All aliens who entered the United States before January 1, 1982, and have lived in the country continuously since they entered

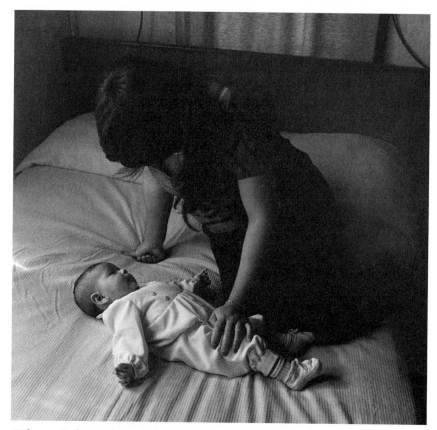

"Blanca," shown here with her four-month-old son, is married to a legal Mexican alien in Del Rio, Texas. Blanca crossed the border illegally after January 1, 1982, so she is not eligible for amnesty and faces deportation.

can apply for legal status. After five years they can apply for citizenship and will be eligible for federal benefits such as welfare, health care, and food stamps.

—Illegal aliens who worked in agriculture for at least ninety days between May 1, 1985, and May 1, 1986, can apply to become legal temporary residents in the United States. After two years as temporary residents, they can apply for permanent residence and be eligible for citizenship in three years.

The bill also specifies increased funds for the Border Patrol and $1 billion a year for four years to help states where large numbers of new legal aliens will strain public assistance budgets. But the landmark provisions of the law are those calling for amnesty for many illegal aliens and civil and criminal penalties against employers who knowingly hire illegal aliens.

The theory behind employer penalties is that if employers are afraid to hire illegal aliens, they will stop coming to the United States to find jobs. But many people think that hope is futile and that the new law may even cause increased illegal entry. Aliens may come, they say, in the hope that the amnesty law will in time be changed to include them or that they can buy fake documents to prove they were in the United States before January 1, 1982.

"I voted for the measure," said Representative James Scheuer of New York, "but I did so with great reluctance, because I fear it will open the floodgates for further illegal immigration."

Henry Cisneros, Hispanic mayor of San Antonio, believes that the immigration bill is not going to solve the problem of illegal aliens. "The problem will continue," he says, "as long as Mexico stays poor and the United States remains rich."

Some persons concerned with the new law expect a huge increase in the use of fraudulent documents. A study carried out in Houston recently showed that two out of every three illegal aliens in the survey already had acquired false identification documents, which they could buy for between $10 and $20.

Texas Senator Phil Gramm, who opposed the bill chiefly because of the amnesty provision, said that he feared a massive use of false documents by people trying to prove that they had lived in the United States since before the amnesty cutoff date of January 1, 1982. Even Senator Alan K. Simpson, one of the sponsors of the new immigration bill, admitted that "document fraud is already a cottage industry in America."

Farmers and agricultural companies are especially concerned about the new law. The amnesty provision for illegals who worked in agriculture may help, and another part of the law says that temporary agricultural workers can be brought legally from other countries if need for them can be proved. But getting them in time to pick crops that must be harvested quickly is a great worry to farmers and

Eliosa Navaez, who has lived as an illegal alien in Del Rio and other Texas cities for the past twenty years, will apply for amnesty under the new immigration law. Her daughters, Jeannette and Magda, were born in Texas and are already U.S. citizens.

This Mexican woman is an illegal alien living in Washington, D.C.
She is seeking information so that she can take advantage of
the new immigration law.

orchard owners. Other businesses that for years have relied on the cheap labor of illegal aliens are equally worried. These include construction companies, restaurants, motels and hotels, and garment manufacturers.

One thing is certain: for the illegal aliens who are successful in their request for amnesty, life will be different. They will no longer have to hide from immigration officers. They will be able to compete for better jobs, join labor unions, take job training. They will be able to emerge from their shadowy existence and join the mainstream of American life. No one imagines that this emergence will be fast or easy, but it will be possible.

167

Another thing is certain: the border zone will be affected much more by the new law than most other parts of the country. As many as 3 million illegal aliens may apply for amnesty. A majority now live in the four border states, most of them near the border. Approval of their amnesty requests will add millions to the Hispanic majority that already exists on the border. And in time the new legal residents will be able to bring spouses, children, parents, brother and sisters from Mexico under the family reunification provisions of the migration law.

Many other questions remain. How vigorously will the government enforce the new law? How effective can enforcement be, even with an increased INS staff? Can any efficient way be found to evaluate the millions of applicants who are expected to ask for amnesty? Most immigration experts expect years of problems, and perhaps significant changes in the new law.

SIX MONTHS after passage of the new immigration law, Paul and I visited El Paso again. The "rush hour" of illegals crossing the Rio Grande to jobs on the U.S. side of the river still took place every morning. This human flow was somewhat reduced, but it was heavy enough to keep the Border Patrol moving fast.

At headquarters, Deputy Chief Patrol Agent Gustavo (Gus) De La Viña showed us some figures. Before the new immigration law was passed, the El Paso Sector Border Patrol was apprehending about twenty-six thousand illegals a month. In December, 1986—after President Reagan signed the bill in October—the number of apprehensions dropped to thirteen thousand. Then the total started going up again and had reached twenty thousand in March, 1987.

We talked to Gus on April 8. "We apprehended 622 yesterday," he said. "On April 7 last year we caught 961. That's a one-third drop," he said, "but it's still a bunch."

I spoke on the phone with Supervisory Border Patrol Agent Ed Pyeatt at the Chula Vista Station in California, where we had been the previous July. He reported a drop in apprehensions similar to

Carried by a simple rubber raft these illegals cross the Rio Grande at El Paso. This is part of the daily "morning rush hour" which sees domestics by the hundreds cross to work in Texas.

that in the El Paso Sector but thought it was much too early to tell what the drop meant in terms of the future.

"We're still averaging twelve hundred apprehensions a day in the San Diego Sector," he said.

Some quick arithmetic told me that would total over 400,000 a year. "Still lots of action on the soccer field?" I asked, referring to the area at the edge of Tijuana where illegals gather before crossing the border into the United States.

"Plenty," Ed said.

All the Border Patrol agents we talked to were taking a wait-and-see attitude toward the new immigration law, but in general there was a feeling that it was a step in the right direction.

"Something had to be done," Chief Patrol Agent Michael S. Williams told us in El Paso. "The message had gone out to the world that if you got past that thin green line, the United States would feed you, educate you, give you a job."

The thin green line that Mike Williams spoke of was the Border Patrol in their olive green uniforms.

Ray Sadler, director of the Joint Border Research Institute in Las Cruces, New Mexico, and an experienced border watcher, agreed with Williams. "It had gotten out of hand, no doubt about that," Ray said, talking to us about illegal entry into the United States. "Congress did the only thing it could."

Bibliography

Books

Arizona: A State Guide (WPA American Guide Series). New York: Hastings House, 1940.

Ashabranner, Brent. *Dark Harvest: Migrant Farmworkers in America.* New York: Dodd, Mead & Co., Inc., 1985

_____ . *The New Americans: Changing Patterns in U.S. Immigration.* New York: Dodd, Mead & Co., Inc., 1983.

California: A Guide to the Golden State (WPA American Guide Series). New York: Hastings House, 1939.

Dobyns, Henry F. *The Papago People.* Phoenix, Ariz.: Indian Tribal Series, 1972.

Hansen, Garth M., ed. *Teaching About International Boundaries.* Las Cruces, N.M.: Joint Border Research Institute, 1985.

Lavender, David. *California: Land of New Beginnings.* New York: Harper & Row, 1972.

Miller, Tom. *On the Border.* New York: Harper & Row, 1981.

Muller, Thomas and Thomas J. Espenshade. *The Fourth Wave: California's Newest Immigrants.* Washington, D.C.: Urban Institute Press, 1985.

New Mexico: A Guide to the Colorful State (WPA American Guide Series). New York: Hastings House, 1940.

Texas: A Guide to the Lone Star State (WPA American Guide Series, first edition 1940, revised edition by Harry Hansen, ed., 1969). New York: Hastings House.

Trimble, Marshall. *Arizona: A Panoramic History of a Frontier State.* New York: Doubleday & Co., 1977.

Articles and Reports

Allard, William Albert. "Two Wheels Along the Mexican Border." *National Geographic*, May, 1971.

Babbitt, Bruce. "We're Neglecting Mexico." *Miami Herald*, June 2, 1985.

Biggar, Jeanne C. "The Sunning of America: Migration to the Sunbelt." *Population Bulletin*, Vol. 34, No. 1 (Population Reference Bureau, Washington, D.C., 1979).

Haupt, Arthur. "The U.S. and Mexico's Blurring Border." *Intercom: the International Population News Magazine*, Sept./Oct., 1982.

"Immigration Reform: a Mess on the Border." *Newsweek*, Dec. 22, 1986.

La Frontera: The Story of the Border. A series of articles, some by Gullermo X. Garcia, others by James Pinkerton, that appeared in the *Austin American-Statesman* from April 20 to 30, 1986. The articles were reprinted in a special supplement of the *Austin American-Statesman* dated April, 1986.

Lang, John S. and Jeannye Thornton. "The Disappearing Border." *U.S. News and World Report*, Aug. 19, 1985.

The Role of Higher Education in the Socio-Economic Development of the Paso del Norte Region. A report presented in El Paso, Texas, to the Select Committee of Higher Education, State of Texas, Feb. 27, 1986.

Stepan, Alfred. "Mexico Deserves Full U.S. Attention." *The New York Times*, June 17, 1986.

Thornton, Mary. "Aliens Law to Change Nation, Experts Say." *The Washington Post*, Nov. 28, 1986.

——————— . "A Murder at the Border of No-Man's Land." *The Washington Post*, April 12, 1986.

Index

The Author

Brent Ashabranner's interest in the interaction of different cultures has led him to write such books as *Morning Star, Black Sun*, about the struggle of the Northern Cheyenne Indians to save their reservation from outside encroachment; *Dark Harvest: Migrant Farmworkers in America*; and *Into a Strange Land: Unaccompanied Refugee Youth in America*, the latter in collaboration with his daughter Melissa. *The Vanishing Border* extends his interest to our vital relationship with Mexico.

Mr. Ashabranner has worked in Ethiopia, Libya, and Nigeria for the Agency for International Development and in the Philippines and Indonesia for the Ford Foundation. He was also director of the Peace Corps program in India.

Mr. Ashabranner now lives in Alexandria, Virginia, where he devotes most of his time to writing.

The Photographer

Paul Conklin is the author and photographer of several children's books, including *Cimarron Kid* and *Choctaw Boy*. He has been a Peace Corps staff photographer and has traveled throughout Africa, Asia, and Latin America on photographic assignments. His photographs appear regularly in *The New York Times*, *The Christian Science Monitor*, and other major newspapers and magazines.

Mr. Conklin holds a degree in journalism from Wayne State University and a master's degree in history from Columbia University. He lives in Washington, D.C.